Retronesia

THE YEARS OF BUILDING DANGEROUSLY

Retronesia

THE YEARS OF BUILDING DANGEROUSLY

TARIQ KHALIL

CONTENTS

By **Daniel Ziv**

FOREWORD

Retronesia is the brainchild of Tariq Khalil, and Tariq is an enigma who has led a double life. I first crossed paths with Tariq at a friend's house in Jakarta in 2006. Slim and handsome with dark Indian features, his strong Scottish accent came out of nowhere and hit me like a truck. Though introduced to me as an environmental scientist, Tariq was slaving over a kitchen stove when we first met, frantically preparing a six-course gourmet Indian dinner for a roomful of appreciative guests.

In the ensuing months and years, Tariq and I ended up sharing an apartment in Central Jakarta, which is HOW I came to know first hand of his duplicitous existence.

He had a day job. It involved dressing in formal work attire and leaving the house at exactly 07:30 each morning for a towering but otherwise nondescript office building in Kuningan. Once inside, he'd sit motionless in a cubicle until 17:00 reviewing graphs and charts and writing environmental impact appraisals. But on weekends, the job sent him to inspect prospects in far-flung locations across Indonesia. This is how Tariq began pursuing an entirely different, mysterious agenda.

He was never a natural traveler. "I find travel to be an awkward thing," he once told me awkwardly. "I just don't see the point." Yet reluctantly, due to work, travel he did. Often to remote corners of the archipelago that most people have never heard of, much less visited.

But while Tariq insisted he didn't enjoy traveling, he apparently had a weakness for wandering. It was on these random work trips that he'd stray from official sites and camps to nearby towns and began exploring their backstreets.

In addition to his office-issued field gear like a laptop, hand held GPS device and safety boots, Tariq started bringing along traditional film cameras. His classic, bulky Linhoff and Mamiya field cameras produced some striking early black and white images. It was through these pictures that I became aware of the utterly unique architectural style that Tariq, taciturn yet obsessive, was singlehandedly uncovering. Gradually —month by month, trip by trip — a series of peculiar private residences and incongruous public buildings marked by bold lines, outlandish angles began to emerge along with some enchanting tales.

But in the stories Tariq brought home after each field trip into distant retro landscapes, not all was unfettered romance. It quickly became clear that just simply getting clean shots of his odd buildings was one of his biggest challenges. Anyone familiar with Indonesia knows that the uncluttered is uncommon: nearly every corner is a flurry of activity, so the opportunity for a clean and unobstructed shot of a dwelling was rare.

On a train journey to Bandung, he was pointed in the direction of the once- famous Dutch Planter's Club – the last stand of the elite Dutch community in the mid-1950s. He tried to get the right shot in evening, but too many parked cars blocked the majestic façade. To get a clear shot in the morning, Tariq stayed overnight, commandeered the *satpam* security guards and briefed them to move cars, cordon off the area and block morning traffic – possibly the most exciting night of work that these car park guards had seen in years. The cherry on the cake was the sight of Tariq at first light, leaving his room and sauntering across the car park in pajamas carrying camera and tripod.

Across Java, what had once been prestigious hotels had slowly sunk into infamy, and for survival had become short stay hotels where traveling businessmen would share rooms with local prostitutes. To get that perfect shot, Tariq made several overnights stays. With conspicuous camera in hand, he often startled hotel guests, whilst puzzling staff with his fixation on the exterior of their static dwellings rather than the dynamic action going on inside.

In Semarang, Central Java, the cold war icon Apotek Sputnik pharmacy had become so crowded out by food carts and street traders that a clear shot was impossible. He entered into negotiation with the patch leader, ultimately agreeing to a shameless cash payment for each food cart seller in return for to shifting their wares so that he could take a photo, rather than his naïve initial offer of a bulk-buy of *nasi goreng* together with *lumpia*, the city's famed spring rolls.

Knocking on one gate in South Jakarta, Tariq encountered an ex-diplomat's daughter who had grown up on Indian food in east Africa. She yearned for that home cooked Indian experience, and so Tariq bartered, training her maid with an Indian cooking master class while outside the family gardener got busy hacking trees and bushes to clear a shot for his camera.

In Medan, Banda Aceh, Surabaya and deepest upriver Borneo, Tariq met his people - Indians of many varieties and purpose. Sailing upriver to coal mines, he idled in their canteens, often eating dhal as watery and brown as the mighty Barito River along which he travelled on his quest to track down what remained of the timber-built military bungalows in the town of Muara Teweh.

All told, Tariq's relentless mission took this non-traveler to almost 50 cities and towns across the sprawling archipelago - from Sumatra in the west to Papua in the east.

A selection of those locales comprise this book, and the mini-essays contained within not only explain the unique dwellings, but touch on everything from family histories and small town anecdotes to religious and political missions, little known colonial history and the cold war. On the surface it's a book about architecture, but really it's a sweeping portrait of Indonesia at arguably the nation's most tumultuous, flamboyant time.

As a long-time student of Indonesia and a keen observer of its people and places, I naturally admired Tariq's noble aim to discover and document an unknown slice of the country's history and aesthetic. But I'm also an artist, and it was the artist in me that witnessed in awe Tariq's patient, passionate, obsessive seven-year quest to utterly lose himself in, and then brilliantly capture, this wild period of Indonesia's early architecture.

This fascinating book also illustrates how connoisseurship thrived in the 1950s, whereas true connoisseurs are a dying breed these days. Through his labor of love *Retronesia*, Tariq Khalil pays beautiful tribute to connoisseurs of the past, and in doing so has earned a rightful place in their milieu.

—

Daniel Ziv directed and produced *JALANAN*— an award-winning feature-length documentary on Indonesia, and is the author of *Jakarta Inside Out* and *Bangkok Inside Out,* and founding editor of the popular urban monthly *Djakarta – the City Life Magazine.*

INTRODUCTION

I came to Indonesia on holiday some ten years ago and *dangdut* music was that trip's soundtrack. Captivated, I dissected this new music in my head; familiar Asian vocalizations, Bollywood beat, meandering flutes and fuzzy electric guitars screaming bad hairstyles and flares. When I began to relax and just listen, this extraordinary music settled down and simply became Indonesia. A few years later I moved to Jakarta and had *dangdut* flashbacks when I came across vintage buildings from the 1950s and 1960s. Here was another shameless fusion of unlikely elements, which when crafted together looked fabulous. This time it was architecture with attitude; vaguely familiar American-style buildings at large in tropical Indonesia.

With a healthy dislike of travel and no understanding of architecture or of my new home I began my therapy. My mission impossible involved annoying scholars and charming aficionados across Indonesia, who led me to fine-looking buildings. I shamelessly talked my way into countless homes– even training a maid to cook Indian food in one. In the company of dispassionate miners and oilmen in eastern Indonesia I often sneaked off aided by *tukang ojek* (motorbike taxi) or other untrained, but finely-tuned eyes to find this *old-new* stuff.

Month by month and trip by trip my collection of buildings, marked by bold lines and outlandish angles, grew. Yet there remained a black hole that had sucked out the life story from these buildings leaving behind just concrete shells. So, with bad *bahasa Indonesia*, I sweet-talked my way deeper inside. Countless doors were graciously reopened and the period's enchanting tales came my way; sometimes the owner, a guard or someone from a *warung* (small restaurant) would share something about this era on the edge of living memory.

The story started around 1950 when Dutch engineers and architects were doing great business delivering endless projects under Indonesia's nation-building push, but were somehow oblivious to Sukarno's post-revolutionary climate. The familiar tropical art deco and the hybridized Indo-European, *Indische* style — popularized in the 1920s and 1930 — were back in vogue. Returning Dutch architects kick-started revivalist architecture: a *Twilight Indies* style exemplified by Jakarta's new town, Kebayoran Baru.

From around 1948 to 1957, while most Dutch architects were busy fashioning Indonesia's old-new look, architects like Ger Boom and Gmelig Meyling took the next step in architectural hybridization. In what were their last years in Indonesia, their imaginations went wild with invention. This *extinction burst* was laden with fresh geometry associated with the carefree aesthetics of late 1940s southern California. The American post-war spirit responsible for introducing car culture, fast food drive-ins and flamboyant motels had a mid-century modern proxy in Java, now appropriately called *Jengki* (after Yankee).

The first fruits of this tropical modern experiment feature in Usmar Ismail's film *Tiga Dara* (Three Maidens, 1956). Beautifully restored, scenes from Kebayoran Baru epitomize architectural innovation and futurist glamour in real time, where art deco and the Indies style were given bold, but playful reworkings.

Art Deco revival, the Menteng Cinema J.M. Greonewegan mid 1950s, Jalan HS Cokrominoto, Jakarta. Image courtesy of Scott Merrillees collection.

Typical *Indische* styled townhouse early 1950s Kebayoran Baru, Jakarta. Image courtesy of KITLV.

Yet the film's optimism seemed oblivious to Sukarno's geopolitical twists and turns to economic independence. By late 1957 society was in flux; the Dutch were forced out and their assets nationalized. Ripples from their expulsion disturbed dormant, but more volatile class tensions. The intricate web of storytelling in Mochtar Lubis' novel *Senja di Djakarta* (Twilight in Jakarta) captures this web of conflicts, compromises and everyday corruption. Written in jail, its dark notes depict a heartless new world that was failing to share the good times promised by Sukarno's Asia-Africa axis.

The windfall from the Netherland's Nexit of 1957-58 created overnight millionaires and refreshed old world elites. With so many assets floating around, a mini building boom took place, but this new phase of modern architecture would be the domain of local building contractors (or *aannemer*). These newly appointed, but anonymous style ambassadors began to monopolize design and build for both ordinary and prestige projects. Little was prescribed or sacred during their aesthetic *merdeka* (independence): engineers, builders, assistants, a few architects — and sometimes owners — added Jengki twists to villa, hotel, office, factory, shophouse, church, and even graves. These sites gave cities and towns modern sophistication and glamour. This was for many just part of *zaman atom* (atomic age), when modern Indonesia's ambitions and self-assertive path rang loud and raised alarm in Western capitals.

The futurist 50s-styled Ministry of Plantations, Gm. Meyling & NEDAM 1955, Jalan Imam Bonjol, Jakarta. Image courtesy of NAI Rotterdam.

Some five years later, the Soenarto villa, Oei Tjong An, 1961 Jalan Kolonel Sutarto, Solo.

Fast forward a couple of generations and we are left with abandoned villas in cities and towns and unloved resorts in the rainclouds. Yet with the help of experts or through chance encounters on the road, I discovered that these were more than just once elegant buildings. I began to see these as cultural monuments buried not by earth and ash, but by simple disinterest. The cultural legacy of an ultra-creative window is the subject of *Retronesia*.

Stories abound, from last orders at the clubhouse built by oblivious Dutch planters in Bandung to the successes of *batik* entrepreneurs in Solo. These and more are all part of a hidden tapesty of tales where threads of daring and risk defined the lives and times of these distant dreamers and mavericks. Whilst these instigators have long departed, their marvellous oddities somehow endure – in a fast-changing Jakarta and beyond.

Highpoints of many childhoods, surviving treasures and forgotten characters are urgently waiting to be rediscovered by a new generation. *Retronesia* has become my *Urban Archaeology for Beginners*. This archaeology does not require expensive expeditions to remote areas, nor shopping for new equipment, all-weather clothing or expert training: interest and passion are all you need to discover something truly magnificent.

JAKARTA & WEST JAVA

The mid-century modern alongside the conventional
Indies styles, Ger Boom Job & Sprey circa 1952,
Jalan Martimbang VI, Kebayoran Baru, Jakarta.
Image courtesy of KITLV.

Former Shell duplexes, Ger Boom Job & Sprey
ca.1952, Jalan Pakubuwono VI, Kebayoran Baru,
Jakarta. Image courtesy of KITLV.

Alternative view of former Shell duplexes, Ger Boom Job & Sprey circa 1952, Jalan Martimbang VI, Kebayoran Baru, Jakarta. Image courtesy of Rizka Fitri Akbar SA Films & Perfini.

Kebayoran Baru Selection
Jakarta

A novel architecture for the new Indonesia began somewhat accidentally way back in the late 1930s. Dutch planners sitting in Batavia, oblivious to impending war clouds of revolution, dreamed up Kebayoran Baru, a satellite town for the colonial capital, but with a difference. Some progressive ideas had seeped during the 1920s and 1930s. One of these was the European Garden City movement, aided and abetted by hands-on Christian socialists dreaming of more enlightened ways of living.

As early as 1946, a year after Japanese rule ended, the Dutch professional class trickled back into the city to build the new town. Indifferent to the post-revolutionary climate under Sukarno's nation-building, they also made the most of the early blueprints for Indonesia's emerging institutions. By 1948, with peace uncertain, Dutch developer Centrale Stichting Wederopbouw had bought up tracts of scrub and orchard from hard up, but reluctant, Betawi orchard holders just beyond Jakarta's unruly southern frontier. Hundreds sold up after accepting compensation and resettlement.

With a nascent, but sizeable civil service, housing was urgently needed in Jakarta. This swayed the government to buy into Kebayoran Baru in early 1949. Paying the developer the princely sum of Rp 15 Million, it took over building Indonesia's first new town. Many resettled civil servants did not adapt well in their new homes and the momentum for building lower-income housing declined. Higher returns encouraged the building of villas for the wealthy.

Elite quarters laid out with multi-storey villas attracted executives from international firms like Shell Oil's Bataafsche Petroleum Maatschappij, Indonesia's primary oil producer. Dutch firms

Classic townhouse
Gm. Melying and Kondor 1954,
Jalan Wijaya, Kebayoran Baru,
Jakarta. Image courtesy of
NAI Rotterdam.

Now demolished New Zealand Insurance Company, Harry Kwee and Job & Sprey 1954, Jalan Wijaya Kebayoran Baru, Jakarta. Image courtesy of Harry Kwee.

dominated construction with prime contractor NEDAM and bureaus such as Kondor, Himalja, IEC and AIA designing new town properties. Engineers and architects sought aesthetic safety through revivalist styles of architecture. The look popularized in the 1920s and 1930s was back in vogue as returnees indulged in the familiar tropical Art Deco and the hybridized *Indische* villa styles.

Many upscale townhouses or *Rumah Partikular* stood out with an alternative geometry. An exuberant new look, echoing America's postwar suburbs was appropriated by style pioneers like Belitung Island

born Gerardus Boom, director of Archtectenbureau Job en Sprey. Around 1952-1953, he designed two small terraced duplex villas for Shell. Harry Kwee, an intern for Boom in 1954 recalled that these were not to everybody's taste, yet this new style was Indonesia's *black swan* and over the next 15 years sprang up all across the country.

Beginning in the late seventies, many gained the right-to-buy in Kebayoran Baru. This new ordinance coupled with high land taxes encouraged much selling and demolition of original properties. That vintage social mix quickly withered as virtually all remaining

low-income properties and much prized green space vanished. Along with its older cousin, Menteng, this is the country's most expensive real estate. The core ideals of the Garden City movement – nurturing the best of city and countryside to balance a social mix reside in the realm of the mythical. Kebayoran's true legacy was the test bed for innovation; its homes, shophouses and public buildings virally inspired heaps of unknown builders, owners and adventurers in places far from Jakarta. Catch this fading majesty and legend of social engineering while you can.

A classic townhouse last used
by the Jakarta municipality,
Jalan Sunan Ampel,
Kebayoran Baru, Jakarta.

Classic townhouse, Ger Boom Job & Sprey 1954, Jalan Sultan Hasanuddin, Kebayoran Baru, Jakarta.

Former Soviet
embassy townhouse
mid–1950s,
Jalan Sriwijaya,
Kebayoran Baru,
Jakarta.

Townhouse entrance detail showing original USSR embassy signage.

Typical bank bungalow unit circa 1959, Jalan Deposito, Jakarta. OPPOSITE: Details of bungalow variations.

Bank Indonesia Estate
Jalan Deposito Jakarta

Bank Indonesia was founded in 1953 as the colonial De Javasche Bank finally shut its doors. The new central bank was allocated a sizeable plot for staff housing in Pancoran, the new city frontier. This out of the way district's consolation was the newly constructed, but relatively traffic-free highway Jalan Gatot Subroto, funded by the USSR, the Swiss and the US.

Like many public institutions of that era, housing was an important benefit-in-kind for staff. Between 1959 and 1961, the bank built around 300 bungalows and larger townhouses for its senior management in newly cleared Pancoran. The bank's bungalows were based on a simple cut-out design; single-storey bungalows with precast geometrically decorative screens and signature tilting verandas overlooking

small gardens. They complemented the design sense of the Bank's new Jakarta headquarters. In style, these bungalows surpassed the vast bulk of its regional offices built in later years. The low-rise estate remains largely intact – a remarkable sight in modern day Jakarta.

View of the Lubis family home.

The Lubis children at home, circa 1968. Image courtesy of the Lubis family.

The Diplomat's Villa
Jalan Tebet Barat Raya, Jakarta

When the 4th Asian Games finally came to Jakarta in 1962, families displaced by construction of the Senayan athletic complex had been resettled in the new suburb of Tebet. Swampland bounding the cities southern and eastern edges was then known as *tempat jin buang anak* (lit. dumping ground for children of genies) an unlikely home for a first-generation diplomat – Pak Haluddin Lubis.

Born to a humble Mandailing Batak family in the highlands of North Sumatra, Pak Lubis had always longed to travel westward in the hope of studying at Cairo's Al-Alzhar University. During the 1930s he got himself on board a ship that took him as far as British India, where he began his studies at the anti-colonial Deobandi Islamic school – a peer of Al-

Courtyard and front verandah doors with period decorative grilles.

Alzhar. Amidst the chaos of 1947 he was evacuated from Delhi to Karachi and found himself in the newly created country of West Pakistan. It was here that he accidentally embarked on a diplomatic career with Indonesia's fledgling Foreign Service.

Like most civil servants he did not draw a large salary, but he sought out honest ways of making money by reselling highly valued foreign products like cameras, projectors, and even cutlery. Reselling a new Fiat 1100 procured in Poland, he purchased the ready-built Tebet house in 1965.

The villa was not part of a complex nor aimed at high-ranking government officials, rather it was speculative; built by an *aannemer* who had bought and developed several land parcels. With Tebet's shady reputation, well-to-do families shunned the area and plots took many years to sell.

Built with Betawi influences, the villa featured a large courtyard with front and back exteriors adopting the then latest designs. Its lower walls were clad in rock and its floral window grilles display period decoration. A tilted veranda provided shade and cross-ventilated lofty ceilings cool interiors - doing away with the need for air conditioners.

With relentless development, the villa is now one of Tebet's few surviving period classics. It has become a unique sight, at odds with the adjoining apartments and adapted commercial premises. Pak Lubis'daughters still live there and remain deeply attached to their home.

Villa Jatinegara

Jalan Kali Jatinegara Barat Raya, Jakarta

The suburb of Jatinegara grew from Meester Cornelis, a market town located about 15 km southeast of Kota (old town Jakarta). Like Tanah Abang and Pasar Senen, Jatinegara was one of the area's oldest markets or *pasar*. It had cultivated a mixed neighborhood, simultaneously home to Balinese, Eurasian, Arab and Betawi communities.

Like all *pasar*, it tenders the same daytime disorder; streets choked by loitering *angkots* (public minivans) and throngs of vendors spilling onto its main roads. From street level, fragments of Jatinegara's past can just about be discerned. Occasional lopsided shophouse roofs are still distinguishable, remnants of its age-old *Pecinan* or Chinatown shophouse settlement.

This out-of-town classic was inspired by what had gone on in Kebayoran Baru. Bold oblique angles carving out an asymmetric exterior are accentuated by a pinched waistline. An extreme curve meets a single column to create the verandah. The villa remains surprisingly unaltered, years after the original family moved up and out. It was used as a wholesale space until the 1990s. Now empty, it is one of the last period buildings likely to morph into another indistinguishable block.

Verandah detail of the Padang villa, Jalan Dadali, Bogor.

Padang Villa
Jalan Dadali, Bogor

Bogor, now a busy southern suburb of metropolitan Jakarta, was first named *Buitenzorg* (without a care). A home-from-home for many Governor Generals and first president Sukarno. Almost 200 years ago, the city hosted the colony's first botanical gardens. A string of scientific research institutes were founded relying on science to keep export commodities such as rubber, cocoa, quinine and tea ahead. With abundant research emanating from its technical schools, Bogor was transformed into a hub for knowledge and manufacturing.

After Independence, exclusive housing in the vicinity of the Goodyear tire factory was developed to satisfy the upper-middle class, intellectuals and businessmen. Hidden behind foliage is a lone-standing classic built for a businessman from Padang in the early 1970s. Following in the 1950s-style fashion, its distinctive corrugated canopy creates a deep recessed verandah. Its window grilles were decorated with ornamentation depicting West Sumatran pastoral scenes and stacked slate rather than conventional stone cladding ornament walls and columns.

After the original family moved to Jakarta, the house stood vacant for many years. Recently, it was converted into an after-hours tutoring college.

Entrance to rear garden with Art Deco-styled gates.

LEFT: Minang pastoral window grille work. RIGHT: View of living room prior to renovation.

Front elevation of BPI and its 1995 renovated facade, Jalan Juanda, Bandung.
OPPOSITE LEFT AND RIGHT: North and south perspectives of the symposium hall.
Images taken circa 1956 courtesy of NAI archive, Rotterdam.

BPI Universitas ITB
Jalan Juanda, Bandung

In 1995 the Bandung Institute of Technology celebrated two anniversaries; the country's 50th anniversary and 75 years of providing advanced technical education. To mark the event, the university commissioned a fresh façade for its Balai Pertemuan Ilmu (BPI) building. A commemorative marble plaque, lauding the *dinamika dan kreativitas* (dynamics and creativity) of the makeover buried the story about a progressive Dutch institution – a soft casualty of decolonization

In 1850, the Koninklijke Natuurkundige Vereeniging (Royal Dutch Physical Society in the Dutch East Indies) was founded. Under royal patronage, scientific learning and scholarship were increased shifting the locus from Bogor and its Botanic gardens. A century later, coinciding with Independence, the society rebranded as the Perhimpunan Ilmu Alam Indonesia (Indonesian Society for Natural Sciences). One of its planned contributions towards nation building was to broaden high school student interest in the natural sciences which then were not as highly regarded as engineering or medicine.

Feeling confident about its worthy position, in 1955 the society commissioned Gmelig Meyling, the leading architect of the day. He worked with building contractor Boen Kiet Lim to create an altogether futurist symposium hall. Like many of Meyling's public buildings, BPI has a monumental feel with a mere three floors. The interior organization is perfectly symmetrical, with a centre opening, twin staircases, parallel spaces and *brise-soleil* appended at each end. Meyling's favoured squares are everywhere; on windows, walls, doors, floor tiles and ventilation openings. The centered balcony is a square-within-a-square.

Like the Societeit Concordia, the former planter's clubhouse in Bandung — another of Meyling's fine creations — the symposium hall was one of countless buildings handed over to the new Republic shortly after its completion. The Society was soon re-organized to eventually become LIPI, the national science institute. The old hall now serves ITB's mission of providing scientific education and research.

BPI foyer with doorway to north entrance and staircase to upper floors.

Interior of the symposium hall with original square panelling and wrap round post and beams.

Oblique view of the Merdeka campus building.
OPPOSITE LEFT AND RIGHT: Details of courtyard and corridor.

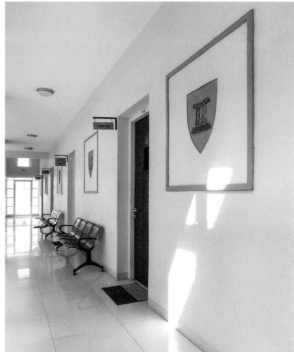

Unpar Merdeka Campus
Jalan Merdeka, Bandung

For the Catholics of Indonesia, the 1950s signalled the start of a race to host the nation's first Catholic u niversity. The Akademi Perniagaan was established in Bandung in 1955 on land donated by the Ursuline Sisters with some financial assistance from Rome. Growing quickly, it became the Parahyangan Catholic Institution of Higher Learning. Its name change reflected a prevailing mood of nationalism; many new Catholic institutions avoided Dutch and Latin names and showed preference towards Javanese-Sanskritic titles.

During his exile in Flores, President Sukarno had enjoyed the hospitality and intellectual exchange proffered by Catholic priests; he learned to recite the Lord's Prayer in Dutch. In time he developed close ties to organized Catholicism, whose mass

Detail of university entrance and upper floors.

LEFT TO RIGHT: Staircase, upper floor corridor, and period lighting in the main hall.

organizations were influential during the post *Merdeka* (independence) era. Unsurprisingly President Sukarno conferred the school university status in 1961, setting it on a steady path to become one of Indonesia's leading private universities.

The new campus was built on Jalan Merdeka around 1957 but surprisingly, its designer remains unknown. What is much more certain is the crafting of that transitional style that fused 1950s elements such as its grid-like panels of *brise-soleil* and

brushed sandstone rock cladding with the familiar late Art Deco streamlined form. Still very much in its original state, the campus building reflects a sense of purposefulness –befitting for what remains a prestigious seat of learning.

Hegarmanah Villa
Jalan Hegarmanah, Bandung

Hegarmanah, Sundanese for 'happy heart', was developed as a hillside residential district after Independence. Home to a new military academy, the area enjoyed relative security as the Islamic insurgency of the 1950s and early 1960s seethed around the city. Hegarmanah slowly began to attract sizeable mansions, villas, and town houses; a new rival to Dutch era districts downtown.

Boen Kwet Kong was among several city builders who created modernist properties here during the late 1950s and early 1960s. With its sloping canopy counterbalanced by the stacked stone pilaster, this distinctive villa was built in the mid-1960s by a Javanese building contractor. Though not formally trained as an architect, Sayogja had worked with many and was a typical learned-on-the-job professional. Being a successful contractor, he bought land in Hegarmanah and built his family home to equal the style and sophistication of surrounding properties.

Foreign aviation experts from Britain, Spain, and America were brought to Bandung during the late 1970s under President Suharto's plans to grow the aviation industry. Entrepreneurs began building upscale houses for rent around Hegarmanah. This drew in the city's first posh supermarket, built just south of Hegarmanah. Exotica such as breakfast cereals, Hershey's chocolate, bacon, wine and cheese changed local tastes forever.

Bought for a reasonable cost just before the spike in property prices, the new owners used money saved to make more rooms for their growing family. They then turned their attention to fixing the building's key feature, its slanting canopy. Thinking that it was a defect, they chopped off much of its hanging ledge. The owners now laugh when they are reminded that for years the architectural verve of the house was the very feature that they had once tried to correct.

The striking entrance of the former nursing school.
OPPOSITE LEFT AND RIGHT: View of the listing north wing with its decorative sequence of circular windows and portals. View of the portico on the southern wing.

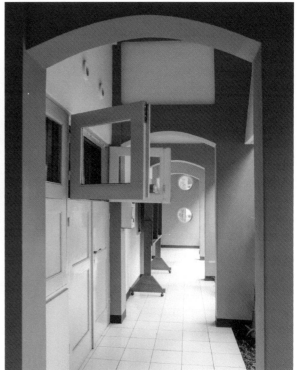

Poltekes
Jalan Prof. Eykeman, Bandung

With fewer than 1,000 doctors and about 3,500 nurses, the sovereign state of Indonesia inherited a weak healthcare system at Independence. In 1951 the new nation's three medical schools managed to produce all of 30 doctors. Yohanes Leimena, the first Minister for Health, introduced a healthcare policy. His "Bandung Plan" was ambitious; to build public health infrastructure and train medical personnel through village polyclinics and local health centres. Trialled in Bandung, which had a relatively good public health system, Leimena's plan was rolled out that decade, but poor organization and funding led to eventual abandonment.

In the former Dutch enclave of Bandung stands a striking period building dedicated to improving the nation's health; a school for training nurses. This

Listing entrance to the dormitories and offices.

nursing academy, equipped with classrooms and dormitories, was very much high-style. Its lurching portico ushers visitors through two parallel wings. The low loggia-like walkways on both floors re-enact the ambience of a short shophouse stroll. Art Deco motifs like *faux* portholes make their appearance, but the 1950s style prevails, in particular the facade's affected off-keel aspect.

Just as with Leimena's health plan — revived in the late 1960s with the setting up of thousands of *Puskesmas* or community health centers — the elegance and spirit of the building endures.

View of the south wings and entrance.

A restored Boen villa from the late 1950s, Jalan Hasanudin, Bandung.

Oblique view of Gereja GKI,
circa 1958, Jalan Kebun Jeruk
Bandung. OPPOSITE: Interior views
of church altar and entrance.

Boen Kwet Kong Feature
Bandung

In the late 1800s, new industries were started in Bandung to process plantation commodities drawing in Chinese migrants to the city. Apart from traders and merchants, sizeable groups of artisans, craftsmen and builders ventured inland bringing with them fresh expertise to West Java's new boomtown. The Boen family left their mark starting with colonial era building work.

Boen Sioej Tjoe (1854 -1918) arrived in Bandung during this upturn. His building business was a success, notably landing the commission for the prestigious Hotel Surabaya. The next generation headed by Boen Joek Sioe (1887-1961), helped the city earn the appellation *Paris Van Java* with abundant Art Deco or tropical modern styled commercial and private buildings. Boen Kwet Kong (1912 -1998), the third generation brought the latest 1950s style to Bandung.

Boen Kwet Kong had learned the family business but was also schooled by Wolf Schumacher and Luchten at the Technische Hogeschool that became the prestigious ITB University. He opened his own bureau and, as was the norm, worked as both architect and builder to the likes of the luminary modernist Meyling to service the city's post *Merdeka* building boom. Demand for his work increased during the late 1950s coinciding with the departure of the Dutch population from Indonesia. Boen applied the modern style treatment effortlessly to create villas, churches, shophouses, commercial

Renovated Boen villa now cafe,
Jalan Siliwangi, Bandung.

properties and leisure facilities. His treatment was versatile; at times building forms were mild adaptations of Art Deco styles whilst others were thorough reworkings of American mid-century modern standards.

The Boen clan would inaugurate their buildings with a traditional Sundanese *selamatan* ceremony at each building site. This custom involved the burial of a coconut, a goat's head and golden nails. Whilst most of Boen's buildings have been altered, a longer lasting homage to his 1950s style *oeuvre* is the family mausoleum he crafted in east Bandung.

Townhouse where Art Deco meets mid-century style, now a Japanese school, Jalan Hasanudin, Bandung.

The Boen Mausoleum, circa 1960s, Cibadak, Bandung.

The Bumi Sangkuriang and Concordia Cub in its near original state, Jalan Kiputih, Bandung.

LEFT AND RIGHT: Details of façade and west wing.

Bumi Sangkuriang Club
Jalan Kiputih, Bandung

The hotel and restaurant Balai Pertemuan Bumi Sangkuriang, located in Bandung's exclusive hillside district of Ciumbuleuit, played a part role in Indonesia's Asia-Africa Conference of 1955. The international conference was held to cement the non-aligned movement and to speed up decolonization. Bandung was a relatively new city.

At the start of the 20th century, its stylish hotels, cafes and boutiques provided imported delicacies and a host of distractions for Europeans seeking respite from Jakarta's heat and humidity. Superior facilities made Bandung the obvious host city for this groundbreaking conference.

Until the 1940s, Bandung's planters and colonial elite would enjoy drinks and dinner at the Societeit Concordia, a fine establishment in the heart of the city, strictly open to *Preangerplanters* or Dutch planters and Europeans. In 1954 President Sukarno ordered the club to vacate its premises so its vast hall could be used for a more serious purpose – hosting Indonesia's first international conference.

LEFT TO RIGHT: The old planters' bar, the billiards room, and changing room with highly styled air brick screen.

As compensation, the club was given some rubber plantation in lush hills overlooking the city. The club approached the city's leading Dutch architect Gmelig Meyling whose firm NV Ingenieurs Bureau Vrijburg produced a modern clubhouse with grounds far removed in style and expression from their former colonial era styled property.

Built along two wings, its dark timbers resemble a hunting lodge. This association is, however, broken by dramatic touches such as a sheared roof with its saddle-bag eave folded over the central bay and a series of white paneled square windows. The club, a coda to Meyling's remarkably creative last 10 years in Indonesia, was completed in early 1957. It was

Meyling's last project in Indonesia, a prelude to mass expulsion and nationalization of all Dutch assets. The renamed club and restaurant is open to the public and Ciumbuleuit has become one of Bandung's most prized addresses.

View of remodeled function hall and ballroom with eagle-shaped pool in foreground.

LEFT: View of original function hall buildings. Image courtesy of the Meyling archive NAI Rotterdam. RIGHT: Construction crew being served lunch, cigarettes, and a soft drink. Meyling in a hat seen leaning over at the left. Image courtesy of the Meyling archive NAI Rotterdam.

CENTRAL JAVA

Front elevation of the Museum Perjuangan, Yogyakarta.

LAHIRNYA INDISCHE PARTIJ DI BANDUNG
TANGGAL 25 DESEMBER 1912
SERANGAN UMUM 1 MARET 1949
DI YOGYAKARTA
TERBENTUKNYA NEGARA REPUBLIK INDONESIA SERIKAT
TANGGAL 17 AGUSTUS 1949
KONFERENSI MEJA BUNDAR
TANGGAL 2 NOPEMBER 1949

ABOVE: Detail of bronze frieze panels depicting key revolutionary events. OPPOSITE LEFT: Detail of canopy sides decorated with Javanese motifs. OPPOSITE RIGHT: Museum interior with artefacts from the revolutionary war.

Museum Perjuangan
Jalan Kolonel Sugianto, Yogyakarta

Yogyakarta was the revolutionary capital of the nascent Indonesian Republic. After independence, the young ruler of Yogyakarta, Sri Sultan Hamengku Buwono IX, felt that a new city museum should commemorate Indonesia's grueling struggle for freedom. Committees were duly formed to judge designs. In mid-1959 IEC from Surabaya had a winning bid costing some 3.5 million Rupiah. Construction lingered for two years before the Museum of Struggle finally opened its doors.

The museum was built around revolutionary symbolism; its 45 windows signified the year of the proclamation of Indonesia's Independence. Heavy bronze relief panels studding the barrel-like exterior curate a selection of heroes and events. Above its modernist layered canopy and squat tapering columns are in-relief Javanese motifs. The outcome was an unlikely fusion, homage to a Buddhist prayer wheel and stupa blended with a touch of flying saucer.

The museum's operation was managed by a diverse committee of artists, public figures, politicians and military personnel. Within two years of its opening, it began experiencing periodic closures partly caused by scant operating budgets. Its fate mirrored that of several private museums which were eventually taken over by the government. The museum closed in the mid-1960s and remained inoperative for two decades. Reopened, it now faces a deadlier struggle; to remain relevant to a new generation.

The mid-century styled Wisma Yatkes, Kaliurang. OPPOSITE LEFT: Art Deco styled villa from the Dutch era now used by Radio Republik Indonesia.
OPPOSITE RIGHT: *Indische*–styled villa now used as a guesthouse by *Kedaulatan Rakyat*, one of the first Indonesian–language newspapers.

Kaliurang Resort
Yogyakarta

Along the zig-zag arc of Java's depleted volcanoes is Gunung Merapi, one of world's most active. Safety alerts often follow the venting of lava and mile-high clouds of grey ash. Merapi's slumbering hillsides are dotted with countless discarded guesthouses (*wisma*) that represent a one time *it* destination.

Merapi is also home to the Kaliurang resort, the Dutch equivalent of the Indian hill station. Kaliurang's first properties were built as temperate retreats for Dutch families and officials. After the revolutionary dust had settled, a new social elite emerged in the 1950s. Java's colonial retreats were not abandoned or torn down like confederate statues, but re-born.

The revived *Indische* and Art Deco styles, which was the standard luxury look of that period, shared space alongside more invigorating forms of 1950s modern architecture. Yet within a generation, tastes in luxurious leisure had moved up the spiral of desire. Nowadays the ski resorts in Korea or Japan are domains for Indonesian elites.

What were formerly exclusive hillside resorts synomymous with luxury were marketed as popular out-of-town destinations to the middle classes. During long weekends and holidays — when Merapi is dormant — the general public flocks to Kaliurang for gatherings, parties and for a more recent leisure interest – the outdoors.

The highly–styled Wisma Hibiscus, Kaliurang.

LEFT AND RIGHT: Details of a classic 1950s–styled villa, now a guesthouse, Kaliurang.

The magnificent St. Ignatius' ceiling.
OPPOSITE: Oblique view of church exterior.

GLORIA IN EXCELSIS DEO

Santo Ignatius Church

Jalan Yos Sudarso, Magelang

In tribute to the founder of the Jesuit Order, the Santo Ignatius Church dates back to the earliest days of the Catholic Mission in Java. In the 1860s, Central Java became pivotal in spreading the newly introduced faith of Catholicism amongst Javanese, Chinese and other non-European communities. In Magelang, during the 1890s, Dutch Jesuits bought land and began building a church complex. In 1962, nearing the centenary of their mission to Java, their

church was revamped. The renovation followed in the wake of the Vatican Council's 1963 ruling that updated liturgical texts and translated sermons into the vernacular.

The renovation was completed in 1965 and based on a simpler modernist style. The interior upstaged the exterior renovation work. The church's ceiling employed a decorative style that was both modernist in spirit and dramatic. A beautiful geometric

sequence on the ceiling partially cascades down both walls – an effect counterpointed by hanging space-age lighting. The choice of graphic style to decorate the ceiling evokes psychedelic patterns popularized in the West during the latter part of the 1960s. Here this decorative solution related to something more immediate – Batik motifs emblematic of central Javanese art.

Verandah and porch of the Soeroso villa prior to renovation.
OPPOSITE: The Soeroso villa during recent renovation work.

Soeroso Villa
Jalan Dr. Soepomo, Solo

Solo has produced some of the finest Batik in Java for many generations. Eminent Batik traders had forged strong links with Solo's nobility whilst other Batik traders coalesced into a political force that aided the Independence Movement in the early part of the 20th century.

Haji Soeroso had started as a humble *Lurik* or blanket maker. He amassed a small fortune after switching his attention to Batik. Soon a Batik magnate with a growing family, he needed a property that could house his children and his enviable social standing.

In the late 1950s work on his townhouse begun. It fused preceding late-era colonial styles with the more fashionable strains of architectural modernism. This new look was expressed by the asymmetric and angular flows of concrete and wood. Oblique geometry–shaped screens and windows; murals and

LEFT TO RIGHT: Detail of murals and an in-built cabinet rendered in the period style located on the villa's upper floor.

recessed furniture are testimony to local craftsmen. An exaggerated 'V' forming pillar and winged canopy lead onto a verandah and living room decorated with teak crafted in the modern style.

Recently it was sold and the manager, seeing its originality, dissuaded the new owner from carrying out demolition plans. Instead it was carefully renovated and is now run as a Javanese restaurant.

LEFT: Teak carved mirror panels in the living room. RIGHT: The airy anteroom with its curving vertical screens and warped pentagram motif to the left.

LEFT TO RIGHT: The Soeroso family circa late 1960s. Image courtesy of Hengky Herendra. Porch with pentagram motif. Entrance to anteroom with the backdrop for the family photo.

White House
Jalan Nuri IV, Solo

Elite 1950s styled villas were a distinguishing feature for *orang berada* (the haves). As land in central Solo was expensive, more modest-sized houses were built attached to one another. In such circumstances façades were the main show-piece. Compared to top-tier villas in the plusher areas of Solo, there was still attention given to style. The revival of the *Indische* era angular archway complimented by a flanging column adds ample modernist flair. The façade makes use of two sets of ventilation holes, one purely decorative whilst the one on the roof was both functional and decorative.

The view from the street.
OPPOSITE: Villa detail from the courtyard.

Soenarto Villa
Jalan Kolonel Sutarto, Solo

This futurist villa was designed in 1961 by Semarang's Oei Tjong An. Construction started the following year, but the owner, Pak Soenarto's business fluctuations led to the project being drawn out over twenty long years.

The finished work, however, remained true to Tjong An's original design and the building is emblematic of his artistry. Sweeping lines, sharp corners, curves and slants reveal an imagination

LEFT TO RIGHT: Detail of exterior work around kitchen and patio.

that may have once glanced over Corbusier's work and ran wild and free beyond his prescriptions. The sci-fi treatment of the exterior was an alien dialect that resounded throughout. It accented windows and entrances, wrapped itself around wood and concrete screens and formed cubicle-like spaces for this leading Solo family. Yet older dialects were still spoken; the round windows and the curving staircase speak of older words made new.

Pak Soenarto passed away in 1977 unable to enjoy the majesty of the finished work. The Soenarto children moved out to start new lives in Jakarta leaving the red gates to open and close for a small business.

LEFT TO RIGHT: Detail of front porch. Styled brick screens in the atrium. View of guest room and teak panelled screen.

LEFT: Main stairwell in the guest room. MIDDLE: Family room immediately behind the guest room. RIGHT: Alternative view of guest room with abundant air brick screens.

Fortress Wisma
Jalan Kolonel Sutarto, Solo

With its wild animal-like stonework skin and fortress-style arrow slits scored up its stairwell, the old *wisma* could have been inspired by defensive fortifications. The modernist multi-storey was a prestigious development, begun around 1960 by an Arab businessman from Solo. Just visible amidst the dense vegetation and dereliction is the once popular V-styled pillar porch.

The owner's dream quickly turned sour when the property fell into enemy's hands after 1965. This was a dark moment in Indonesian history that advanced opportunities to settle old scores, real or imagined. Property, businesses, and land were confiscated by those with the right kind of muscle. Several decades later, the old wisma acquired disputed property status and fell into dereliction. Squatters, vandals, and thieves removed most of its fittings including the once jagged railings on its terraces. If and when the property dispute is settled, the towering landmark will most likely be razed to redevelop its highly valued land.

Front elevation of hotel. OPPOSITE LEFT: Rear extension with added guest rooms. OPPOSITE LEFT: The hotel reception.

Hotel Sinar Indah
Jalan Adisucipto, Solo

Located on a busy highway exiting Solo, Hotel Sinar Indah mimics the postwar American motel. The façade has verve reminiscent of an LA drive-in from the 1950s. Built sometime in the early 1960s as the family house of Pak Sugiarto, a local building contractor, it also served as an office for his business. Throughout the 1970s the building was a landmark on Jalan Adi Sucipto – the major road linking Solo and Yogyakarta. It was sold in the early 1980s to a car dealer who converted it into the Hotel Sinar Indah.

Modest annexes were added, but the building's original exterior remained unaltered as the new owner prized its fragmented pentagonal façade. For a time this was one of Solo's leading hotels, but it failed to keep pace with trends such as boutiques and efficient travel accommodation. It now has a somewhat staid but secure existence catering to the short-stay market.

The facade of Apotek Sputnik. OPPOSITE LEFT AND RIGHT: View of curvaceous counter and cabinets. Counter detail with souvenir foods.

Apotek Sputnik
Jalan Panandaran, Semarang

The supply of western medicines in Indonesia dwindled after the nationalization of foreign pharmaceutical firms in the late 1950s. When available, the sale of western medicine was restricted to select government officials and the well-to-do.

In Semarang, NV Phapros started by the Oei Tiong Ham Concern saw an opportunity in scarcity and began drug manufacture.

A striking new outlet for these drugs was Apotek Sputnik, which debuted in Semarang one year after

the Soviet Sputnik satellite launch of 1957. For the owners the Sputnik name signified the excitement stirred by the space race. Style and sophistication were reflected in the building's architecture. With tablet-making machines rare, powdered medicine

LEFT AND RIGHT: Amorphic panel motif on the main door. Doorway with amorphic motif.

was sold over the counter encased in Sputnik's period packaging. With the flair of a freehand painter, An put his signature sweeping lines and curves to shape the building. The vibrancy of the exterior, with its rocket-cum-satellite above the door and space age windows reveal a highly styled interior. Amoeba shaped windows and perforated cut-outs defining doorways abound. Counters and benches are given a similar cartoon-like treatment.

Even if the space race has made a comeback, today pharmacy chains reign supreme, offering scale and range. The Sputnik is little more than an empty shell lodged between street carts that sell souvenirs and food.

LEFT AND RIGHT: Shelves and window given the space-age treatment. Window detail from the courtyard.

Main view of the Crescendo villa. OPPOSITE LEFT: Furniture-like columns leading to the garage. OPPOSITE RIGHT: Gabled entrance and heavily stylized cut-away verandah.

Villa Crescendo
Jalan Tambanan, Semarang

The Dutch East Indies had its Great Gatsby characters, like Oei Tiong Ham, head of Asia's most powerful conglomerate, the Oei Tiong Ham Concern. He died in 1924 leaving behind eight wives, a collection of mistresses and around twenty children. Indonesia's very first *starchitect* was Oei Tjong An, a child from Ham's inner circle, who received the finest of childhoods money could buy with schooling in Geneva.

Oei Tjong An opened one of Java's few architectural bureaux in Semarang during the 1950s. A feature of Semarang's High Society by day, he worked upper end clients who were looking to him to showcase their status. By night, Oei Tjong An devoted himself to dancing and libation. He was often found networking in Java's exclusive resorts; happy hunting grounds offering rich promise to the well-connected.

Oei Tjong An went beyond his peers such as Lim Bwan Tji and became a successful lifestyle brand during the late 1950s and early 1960s. He astutely spread mid-century modern architecture as the epitome of luxury design. Brazenly promoting himself in Semarang's press, mixing Bahasa Indonesia and English, he berated the work of his peers writing "...*Don't Build without Pride, Why Build Houses So positively ugly, In a spirit of imitation are the work of.... Monkeys.*" Within a decade, he had created a stack of bungalows, palatial villas and commercial buildings for Indonesia's newly-made millionaires.

The Crescendo was a product of these heady times. Like many of his works it was a landmark of luxury in Central Java. Built in 1962 by Yo Tjin Bok, his trusted *Aannemer*, it resembles a sideboard balanced on a ledge. Its simple pitched roof, common to the *Indische era*, villas contrast the profusion of disruptive features; tapered legs create space for the car port, oblique canopy formations define its curving verandah and window bay. Perforated walls and geometric screens create secluded outdoor refuges. The Crescendo typified the lives and aspirations of elite families of the day, but unlike many of its illustrious contemporaries, the Crescendo possessed multi-generational appeal and remains in pristine condition and on standby for the family.

Front elevation of the
Soediro villa.
OPPOSITE: The Soediro
living room.

The Soediro Villa
Jalan Anggrek, Semarang

Not all aspiring villa owners hired architects. In 1962 Soediro, a professor who had previously held the enviable position of Head of East Indonesia Harbors in Makassar, returned home to Semarang and began designing his family residence. Though not an architect, the naturally gifted Pak Soediro was full of creative impulses and the results of his collaboration with a local builder are striking and original.

Deviating from the popular pentagon form, his creation had an unbalanced aspect similar to the Jatinegara villa in Jakarta. Beyond the pinched bialetti moka pot form, he added other twists such as the off-center archway, stonework coating most of the gable and ventilation holes placed eccentrically at waist level.

In the 1960s, the house faced farmlands with views that reached up to the hills south of the city. This tranquil vista vanished during the 1990s, replaced by a towering shopping mall. The Professor passed away in 2002, but his villa continues unchanged as the family home.

Oei Kang Jan villa from the 1960s converted into a cafe, Jalan Menteri Supeno, Semarang.
OPPOSITE: Oei Kang Jan townhouse circa 1962, Jalan Menteri Supeno, Semarang.

Oei Kang Jan Feature
Semarang

From the late 1950s through to the early 1960s, villas built in the latest Western styles were in demand by Semarang's business elite. The rich port city hosted many competing building contractors, engineers and some architects. Top-end clients, those that preferred showy creations, would seek out the likes of Oei Tjong An. For those who considered his fees

and designs too extraordinary, competing designs by civil engineer Oei Kang Jan provided a stylistic but value for money alternative.

After returning from study in America, Oei Kang Jan opened his bureau NV Sapta Pura in the old town. Becoming one of Semarang's leading architectural firms. His works were once abundant in

the heart of new Semarang along Jalan Pandanaran and prestigious new town areas such as Jalan Menteri Supeno. He provided a mix of both showy and minimalist-styled modern villas. A flamboyant survivor is the mansion that is now the Mi Casa nail studio.

Front elevation of the Hadi house, Oei Kang Jan 1962, Jalan Menteri Supeno, Semarang.

LEFT AND RIGHT: Details of the Hadi house interiors.

The Mi Casa nail salon,
Jalan Merak, Semarang.

LEFT AND RIGHT: Detail of Mi Casa's interwoven roof lines, rock cladding, and geometric cut window.

Kopeng Kartika Wisata guesthouse renovated by Oei Tjon An circa 1955.
OPPOSITE: The Kopeng guesthouse after renovation by Ir. H.P. Uittenbogaard.
Image taken in 1952, courtesy of Mark & Bertie Uittenbogaard.

Kopeng Resort
Kopeng

Puncak, Lembang, Kaliurang all the way east to Batu and Selecta in Malang were the first organically chilled luxury retreats. Here Java's implanted elite founded exclusive bolt-holes to create their own temporary make-believe lifestyle. These first-generation properties were ethnically exclusive with smoking chimneys, verdant lawns and tennis courts.

Kopeng, high on Mount Merbabu, was typical of this kind of resort. The good times went up in smoke during the 1940s when it became a battle-ground, changing hands between Dutch delusions and ascendant freedom fighters. In 1949, tranquillity returned when it again became a rest house for Dutch planters and government officials.

By the mid-1950s, Tan Kim Yang saw an

View of the Hotel Amalgamasi complex Kopeng, Oei Tjon An, 1955–1958.
OPPOSITE: End elevation of a hotel bungalow with arching verandah, split roof and stacked rock pilaster.

opportunity and purchased Kopeng. Ignoring night-time curfews he embarked on a venture to upgrade the mountain resort as a destination for Semarang's business community, who had replaced the Dutch and Eurasian high society. He called on the services of architect Oei Tjong An who went to work renovating the resort's original mansion and transforming the grounds with fifteen or so vibrant bungalows. He recreated the mid-century modern desert lodge style aided by the abundant use of butterfly roofs, tilting beams, fancy trellises and rock work. Palm Springs had made a guest appearance in age old Java.

Trouble returned to Kopeng when its ownership was challenged. The army took over the resort in 1959. Soon marketed to the general public, popular stage performers were brought up for weekends. For later generations of the well-off, interest in Kopeng vanished. Several properties were donated to the Catholic clergy, but most properties remain shuttered, relics from good times past their high point.

WIJAYA KUSUMA

Wisma Wijaya Kusuma and Wisma Wungkul Kopeng,
seen from the tennis court, Oei Tjong An, 1955–1958.

Detail of Wisma Wijaya Kusuma, Oei Tjong An, 1955–1958.

LEFT AND RIGHT: Interior and exterior detail of Wisma Wungkul with its trellises, striped patterning and geometric windows.

Vila Peny Kopeng with its woven timber trellises, Oei Tjong An, 1955–1958.

The desert lodge styled Villa Sejuk Segar Kopeng with its distinct stacked rock pilaster, Oei Tjong An, 1955–1958.

EAST JAVA

Oblique view of Wisma Jendral Achmad Yani, Gresik.

Detail of Wisma Achmad Yani canopy and main *brise–soleil* panel.

Wisma Jendral Achmad Yani

Jalan Veteran, Gresik

In 1955 the United States Government provided a loan to develop Indonesia's first national cement company in Gresik, an old Javanese port town rich in limestone. This plant would end the monopoly enjoyed by the Dutch–owned Padang Portland Cement Maatschappij and lift the nation's burgeoning spirit of self-reliance.

Seven years after cement production had begun; the company inaugurated a magnificent public hall – the Wisma Semen Gresik. On first take, the hall appears in the streamlined Art Deco cut. A closer look reveals brazen hybridization. The exterior façade supports several overlapping porticos each with a waving canopy. Stained glass windows recall European

Art Nouveau, whilst three panels of *brise-soleil* use decorative mid-century geometrics. Studding the lower walls, eleven amorphic stone reliefs debut socialist-realist styled milestones of the nation building story.

The interior is simply striking. Large paneled murals painted in the western decorative art forms

Detail of eastern entrance of Wisma Achmad Yani.

popularized in the 1960s create a festive atmosphere. The artist Sapto Hoedojo, son-in-law of Indonesia's renowned artist Affandi, painted this impressive wrap-around gallery of murals depicting the energy and atmosphere of far-flung archipelagic ceremonies.

With the advent of the New Order, the hall was renamed Wisma Achmad Yani in 1966 in tribute to the murdered army general. Whilst its cousin, the sports stadium, was mothballed years ago, the hall remains in public use, providing a prized space for functions and weddings. Semen Gresik became Semen Indonesia in 2013 and is the country's largest cement producer.

Sapto Heodojo's vibrant balcony mural heavy with 1960s style abstraction.

Sapto Heodojo's interior murals.

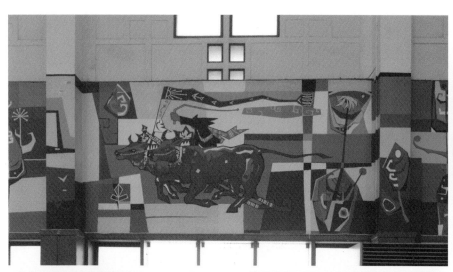

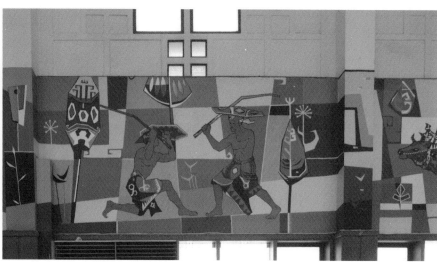

CONTINUED: Sapto Heodojo's interior murals.

Portico decorated with irregularly-cut bronze bas-reliefs with their somber grey patina.

Detail of the 11 bas-reliefs resonant of the socialist-realist style.

The main gate of the Stadion
Semen Gresik with its bold
fusion of Art Deco and 1950s
modernism.

The Fusion House
Jalan AKS Tubun, Gresik

Joint ventures between Chinese traders and local royalty go way, way back and were instrumental in establishing port cities or *entrepots* in the archipelago. In time these *entrepots* dotted the northern shores of Java from Tuban, Gresik and Surabaya in the east, to Sunda Kelapa (now Jakarta) and Banten in the west. Foreign merchants from ports in China, India and Yemen settled in Gresik giving the old town a cosmopolitanism texture. Around the late 1400s, at the zenith of the Hindu Majapahit Kingdom, Gresik became a point of incursion for Islam into Java.

Post-independence, Gresik morphed into a suburban hub for Surabaya. Its narrow old quarters retain original Arab, Dutch, Chinese classic Javanese architectural styles. This particular creation, the product of several fanciful fusions began in 1891 as a traditional Chinese-styled house built by Tan Bian Gwan and Tan Kok Tjing. In 1933 ownership changed hands to Tan Thing Tjom. With ample land at the rear, a lumber works and a two-storey townhouse was added with high ceilinged rooms. The grandson of Tan Thing Tjom, the eldest living resident, recalls that the makeover occurred in the 1960s when a furniture store fronted their home.

Heroes' House
Jalan Ngagel, Surabaya

Almost every Indonesian city has a street named after Hadji Oemar Syaied Cokroaminoto. A century ago, he founded Sarikat Dagang Islam (Islamic Traders Association) which was intsrumental in laying down the roots for Indonesia's nationalist movement. From the ranks of batik cooperatives, a broad mix of ideas flourished; progressive Islam, European inspired modernism, nationalism and various blends of socialism.

Moving to Surabaya, Cokroaminoto started a boarding house that filled with promising students. Here he mentored several future leaders; the young Sukarno, Muso the early leader of the Communist party, Semaoen the trade unionist, and Kartosoewirjo who would lead Darul Islam and its insurgency in West Java. It was here that Sukarno met his first wife, Nonya Oetari, Cokroaminoto's daughter.

Some forty years after their divorce, Sukarno's administration honoured Nonya Oetari with a modest bungalow built by one of the leading building contractors, IEC. In characteristic pentagonal form, it was decorated using latte coloured geometric stonework. Now squeezed between towering multi-storey blocks, it remains the family home. Under its drooping eaves, a dusty marble plaque signifies its proud antecedents. On Independence Day 1961 — from the distance of Jakarta — President Sukarno inaugurated the house with a formal pronouncement:

We, as Indonesians, realize that the nation's patriots have provided meaningful contributions to achieve our Independence. With regards to those contributions, we Indonesians, with great solemnity and honour, present this building as our highest token of appreciation.

The imposing façade of the Salim Martak mansion.
OPPOSITE: The famed living room film set with its characteristic
air-brick screen panels and Arabesque carpets

The Arab Villa
Jalan Untung Suropati, Surabaya

Darmo, an exclusive suburb, was built just south of Surabaya in the early 1920s catering for an ever-growing European population. Like colonial enclaves in Jakarta and Bandung, Darmo took a passing interest in Garden City concepts. Here, wealth equaled an abundance of fine properties built in the latest colonial architectural styles.

The area began to empty of its Dutch residents after 1950, changing the suburb's ethnic makeup. Darmo was put under government control to alleviate a city housing shortage. Changes to the Nationality Laws in 1957 forced the remaining Dutch population to sell up. This made way for new owners, some of whom began making renovations that over time altered the area's look. Despite years of change, some homes still receive utility bills in the names of former Dutch owners.

Salim Martak, a Surabayan Arab had been an early buyer, acquiring a former Dutch Army mess in 1952. By 1963, to house his growing family, he added an extension, choosing the waving roof line and canopy popularized by Hotel Indonesia and the nearby Wisma Achmad Yani in Gresik. It was completed with a scattering of diamond shaped air vents and a brick-like veneer in an all-white finish. This unusual ensemble of elements created an elegant confection. In the 1970s and 1980s, his home was a favored movie set and regularly hosted celebrities and actors.

The Hotel Olympic with offices and shops leading off to the rear.

Hotel Olympic
Jalan Urip Sumoharjo, Surabaya

In the 19th century, Surabaya was a prosperous port metropolis that rightly regarded itself as on a par with the capital. In the early 1950s, it went through a post-war rebuilding program aimed at restoring civic pride - and being at the heart of the Indonesian revolution - honour.

Construction of an international hotel was a necessity, but this constituted considerable expense. A joint venture was set up between businessman Ong Kie Tjay and the city government thereby guaranteeing badly needed funds. The Hotel Olympic and integrated commercial strip was built in 1954; a timely challenger to the city's colonial landmark, the Hotel Oranje (renamed the Majapahit Hotel).

Architecturally in the late Art Deco style, the Olympic became a new era city landmark; its towers could be seen from the nearby island of Madura. A painting hanging in the reception depicts its original streamlined look. Windows on its upper floors, where its restaurant served local and foreign guests, were later sealed and inverted egg-cup canopies added.

This drastic makeover altered what was once a prestigious city institution and somehow symbolized the district's general decline. The arrival of international hotel chains, providing guests with the latest facilities, ultimately sidelined the Olympic. Unable to recover its majesty, this eccentric landmark survives as a short stay hotel, whilst colonial chic prevails at the beautifully restored Majapahit Hotel.

Gelora Pancasila
Jalan Indragiri, Surabaya

Sport was once a soft power tool for advancing Indonesia's plan for a revolutionary world order. In Surabaya, construction of the stadium, Gelora Pancasila, began during the peak of President Sukarno's dangerous years typified by confrontation and brinkmanship. In mid-1966, as President Sukarno watched his power drain away, the new city stadium full of verve was inaugurated by East Java's military Governor.

The stadium's gambrel roof evokes the Dutch townhouse, but this hint of revivalism was offset by the spiky canopy and its arrangement of irregular windows. The foyer was laid out along mid-century lines. Stairs dedicated for VIPs lead to the upper level with a curving bar that once served alcohol. One of its two murals nonchalantly rewrite history by depicting sporting triumphs, starting with Indonesia's participation in the Olympics of 1952, 1956 and 1960, the 4th Asia Games in 1962 and GANEFO or Games of New Emerging Forces held in 1963.

LEFT: Main foyer with ceiling and concrete screen partition rendered in period decoration. RIGHT: Staircase to VIP balcony.

Indonesia was the first country to be expelled by the Olympic Committee after Jakarta banned athletes from Taiwan and Israel from participating in the Asia Games. In response, President Sukarno with Chinese funding set up GANEFO. With its bold slogan — *Onward No Retreat!* — GANEFO promised to be the radical sporting alternative that would play its part in hastening the creation of a fairer world.

In late 1963 GANEFO's sporting events were held in Jakarta attended by 51 nations including several South American states, the newly liberated nations from Asia, Africa and the Soviet bloc.

With Sukarno gone, the Chinese under Mao's leadership quietly wound up GANEFO in 1966 and the Olympic Committee resumed its immense influence over world sport. As economic priorities now took center stage, Indonesia's interest in sport tumbled. Surabaya's once prominent city stadium pays its way servicing less prestigious events like graduation ceremonies. Its interior periodically fills with desks when it becomes a large exam hall for civil servants.

TOP: M. Sidik's mural from December 1965 with sporting history rewritten. BOTTOM: Mural depicting the courage and skill of traditional hunters.

View of the Gelora Pancasila indoor stadium.

The Ampel house and its imposing façade.
OPPOSITE: Ground floor window detail.

Ampel House
Jalan KH Mas Mansyur, Surabaya

Muslim mercantile groups including Malays, Achinese, Bugis, Guajarati Indians, Persians, Yemeni Arabs and the Hui from China have traded in the old port of Ampel for almost a millennium. Five hundred years ago, Ampel expanded beyond trade to become an important locus for the spread of Islam.

It has become known as *Kampung Arab*, a suburb of Surabaya. Despite complete suburbanization, Ampel retains its old hue, drawing Islamic pilgrims by the busload. Souk-like, crammed with small open-air shops selling all manner of goods associated with the Arab world such as dates, pistachios, sultanas, musk and carpets and now fashionable Arab attire.

This two-storey home, a clone of the American mid-century modern style, is on Ampel's busy high street. Though its setting in this pilgrimage district appears incongruous, the street was at one time lined with numerous Indische-style villas reflecting the aspirations of its Arab merchant class. Shortly after Independence, a new style of architecture emerged, reflecting a much sought-after foreignness. In the early 1960s, a local Aannemer built this as a family home for Pak Mohamed Yamin, a Surabayan Indian jeweller. The house's footprint follows the Straits-style Chinese shophouse precepts of narrow frontage and an elongated rear area. A small courtyard and garden provide quarters for women in keeping with the Arab living style.

Model Belanda (Dutch style) is how his children remember their home which then was an evening landmark, where people would congregate to *nongkrong* (hang out) and smoke cigarettes.

Front elevation of the Lawang villa. OPPOSITE: Details of split roof, hanging eaves, richly decorated cladding, air holes, and listing walls.

Lawang Villa

Jalan Sumber Bening, Lawang

On the road to Surabaya is the small, indistinct town of Lawang. In the 1930s, a major botanical garden for agricultural research was founded in the town. Together with Church retreats and tea plantations, Lawang had its very own resort-like character.

Flanking the highway entering the town, stand many abandoned villas once used as getaways by wealthy Dutch families. Their designs show early and late period *Indische* architectural styles. Occasional 1950s styled homes make up this collection of abandoned villas.

Built by local contractors in 1955, this orange-hued villa is one of Lawang's better maintained post-Independence era properties. Its simplicity is achieved by the classic pentagram configuration of the façade. Complementing this form are decorative ventilation holes and a split roof - popular in this part of Java. Despite its small frontage, the house runs deep with nine rooms. Pak Sudikun, the deceased owner had made his career as an army man in nearby Malang. His son cherishes the building's originality and craftsmanship and sees no necessity for alterations.

Oblique view of the Fabrik Tiger with its split roof, elaborate grille work on encased windows and V supported column.
OPPOSITE LEFT: Interior with obliquely cut corridor. OPPOSITE RIGHT: Detail of front porch.

Fabrik Tiger
Jalan Wahidin, Lawang

The Arab community in Indonesia is relatively small but overrepresented in many spheres of public life. Most trace their origins back to Hadrami communities along Yemen's arid southern coastline. The Arab diaspora first settled in East Java's coastal towns such as Pasuruan and nearby Bangkil. From there, Arab traders built up their businesses before venturing inland to towns like Lawang and Malang.

This villa has remained with the family of Pak Fauzi Muhammad, a second-generation Malang-Arab. Around 1963, like many newly styled properties of that period, it was built by local contractors and artisans from Malang. The use of the split ventilated roof, irregular stone work cladding and the V-shaped canopy reflect Malang's mid-century modern style craze. Decorative 1950s flair seep into the interior exemplified by a revived *Indische*–styled arched doorways. In pristine condition, it backs up to a small stonework business, which gives the property its new name and ongoing lease of life.

Front elevation of the villa with its signature maritime porch. OPPOSITE: Rear building with distinctive oblique window on the upper floor. *Indische*-style cladding contrasting with modernist stonework on the ground floor.

The Maritime Villa
Jalan Ciliwung Malang

In the aftermath of the Japanese surrender of August 1945, a revolutionary fervour and sometimes chaos swept across Indonesia. Remembered as *Bersiap* (get ready) hasty plans were made; Indonesian Youth Brigades (*Angkatan Muda Indonesia*) formed arming a generation of spirited volunteers. Many in Malang's Chinese community saw an opportunity to show their patriotism. Siaw Giok Bie and Go Gien Tjwan

LEFT: Louvered windows and circular ventilation holes set above characteristic *Indische* rock cladding.
RIGHT: Windows with Art Deco grille work set around a Javanese pastoral grille framed by modernist rock cladding.

created a local Chinese militia, the *Angkatan Muda Tionghoa* (Chinese Youth Brigade) who played their part in the Battle of Surabaya later that year.

This immaculate villa was built in 1960 by a local contractor for the late Pak Oesman Soegianto. Whilst establishing himself in Malang as a successful merchant, he fought in campaigns against Japanese and later Dutch forces, in time becoming a decorated ethnic Chinese war veteran. His home, however, commemorated his life-changing journey that began when he set sail from Makassar to East Java well before the war. The building's outwardly *Indische* villa form was subtly transformed by a myriad of more contemporary design features, such as oblique cutaway windows, a mosaic of faux portholes, and free-form arrangements of *Indische* period rock cladding. Modernist rock work was hauled to frame a Java pastoral scene on living room windows.

LEFT: Door with oblique glass window pane. RIGHT: The guest room nominally screened by oblique partitioning and Pak Oesman's framed medals to the left.

White period grille work takes a break from cutting diamond geometric sequences to craft a fertile maiden approaching flowing waters. Similar treatments find their way into living areas, most notably the oblique cutaway screen dividing the guest room, making this home a unique late *Indische* hybrid.

The home's focal point is the elaborate maritime themed iron grille with a fish and a sailing ship. This still greets and intrigues visitors, but this symbolized Soegianto's peacetime sea voyage from Makassar all those decades ago. The stanchion formed by the Greek letter λ holds up the canopy that frames the

grille on the porch. This was once a place to sit and view the comings and goings on this upscale street. Unlike what has happened to most of Malang's retro treasures, a love for 'the old-fashioned style' is the simple explanation given by Soegianto's daughter for not altering the family home.

Front elevation of the Sarangan villa.
OPPOSITE: Details from the façade.

The Sarangan Villa
Jalan SaranVgan, Malang

For a relatively new provincial town, Malang boasted a profusion of clubs, societies, newspapers and a flourishing Performing Arts scene on a par with Java's major cities. Though small in number, Malang's Chinese community played a significant part in shaping Malang's vibrant cultural scene. In the 1930s and 40s, astute members of this community had begun resettling in the former Dutch quarter around Jalan Ijen. Whilst these *Indische* era properties in former colonial districts retain their old-world character, the streets around newly established well-to-do quarters surrounding Jalan Sarangan were about the new. Here vibrant modern architecture was the common sight.

This villa stands out with its long-sheared roof and its braided eaves. The grey from Shanghai plaster renders geometric decoration. Windows are shaded by the familiar modernist cut-away canopies. Little is known about the villa's designer, but it was built around 1959 on the request of a Malang Chinese family, then sold in 1964. It is well maintained by the octogenarian owner who has little desire to change her home.

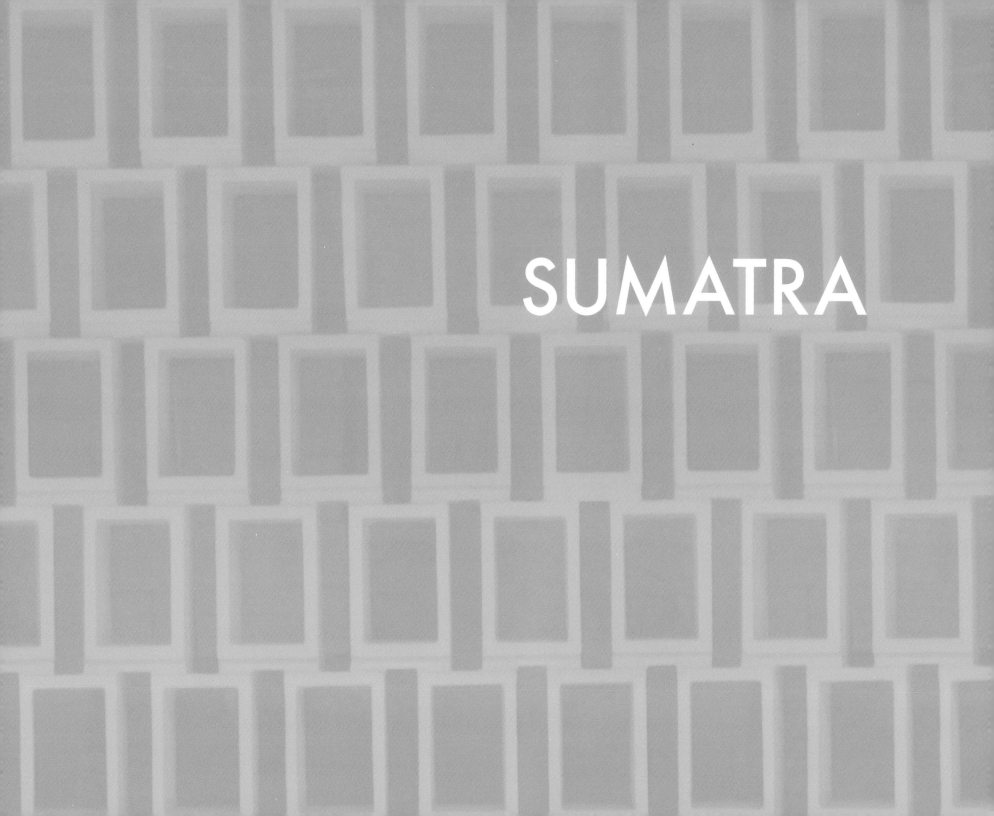
SUMATRA

Oblique view of the banker's villa.

OPPOSITE: Typical gathering in the main living room. Image courtesy of Ibu E. Tanjung.

Banker's Villa
Jalan TD Perdede, Medan

Bank Dagang Nasional Indonesia (BDNI) was founded by pro-Independence businessmen in 1946. Initially operating inside Republican-controlled areas during the late 1940s, it was one of the few Indonesian banks to circulate the Republic's earliest currency, the *Oeang Republik Indonesia*. Headed by Pak Muslim Jalil Harahap, BDNI became licensed as a foreign exchange bank in 1955.

In 1961, Pak Muslim commissioned a big time building contractor to build his family villa. Under his tight supervision, the builder affected the longhouse-like form to contain a large living room

Detail of the honeycomb window sequence.

to entertain guests, an equal sized family room, an office, seven bedrooms, a kitchen and a garage for his three cars. A fluctuating sequence of honeycomb windows and the jagged canopy add distinction. High voided ceilings kept the large guest room cool during frequent gatherings.

Mid-way through the New Order period, BDNI ran into financial turmoil and was acquired by the Gajah Tunggal Group founder Lim Tek Siong, a pepper tycoon from Bandar Lampung. The Asian Financial Crisis of 1997 precipitated BDNI's second collapse and a year later the government suspended the bank. Much to the regret of Pak Muslim's children, the villa recently left family hands and became an office of another bank.

LEFT: Detail of the jagged porch and villa entrance. RIGHT: More of the honeycomb window sequence.

The Medan duplex.
OPPOSITE: Detail of the gabled entrance with textured facia, abstract roof vent and V column supporting a porch.

The Duplex
Jalan Perintis Kemerdekaan, Medan

The Kemerdekaan area in the heart of Medan was first developed for railway housing during the colonial era. Some modernist villas began to enliven the area in the late 1950s and 1960s. From the late 1980s to the early 2000s, classic residential homes from that era and older railway housing were demolished and replaced by featureless multistory shophouses. Over time, newer high-rise properties were built leaving little visible of the area's heritage.

One modernist survivor that breaks this pattern of change is the duplex-styled villa. During that creative free-for-all era, the more outlandish tastes of wealthy home owners were often satisfied by this type of building. Playful features abound from the stone accents that decorate the divided gable, the tear away roofs, oblique windows and the pointing canopy pillar supports. After standing empty for many years, it will likely follow the fate of surrounding properties.

DEKOPIN
Jalan Sei Besitang, Medan

Inspired by the *Budi Utomo* movement's principles of self-reliance, artisans and growers began forming cooperatives during the early part of the 20th century. The role of co-ops in the Indonesian economy was fortified by the Constitution of 1945. They were unified into Dewan Koperasi Indonesia or DEKOPIN, (Indonesian Cooperative Council) in 1947.

A host of factors such as poor administration and irregular funding from the government prevented co-ops from playing a more substantive role in raising incomes and growing the economy. Co-ops were occasionally successful, but more often remained ineffective due their bureaucratic, top-down design.

The Cooperative Council's new regional offices were built in Medan in the mid-1950s. For a run-of-the-mill co-op building, something unusual happened; its two new halls resembled the latest style associated with Medan's well-to-do parts. The bay of geometric canopies over doors and windows create deep overhangs to shade the façade. Even during the hottest parts of the day interiors need no fans or air conditioning.

Aceh Ruko
Jalan Ahmad Yani, Banda Aceh

During the reign of the Acehnese Sultanate, the Peunayong quarter was Banda Aceh's mixed settlement attracting maritime traders from India, China and as far west as the Ottoman empire. As the Dutch battled to subjugate Aceh through the 19th century, they encouraged Chinese merchants and laborers to settle. Peunayong morphed into the city's Chinatown district as arrivals that prospered introduced southern Chinese styled shophouse architecture, first building with timber then in later years with brick and stone. Peunayong's crumbling shophouses — set apart by their characteristic arched walkways — somehow manage to resemble those found in Malaysia and Singapore.

At night the quarter is transformed as lines of food carts move into place concealing the old shophouses. Small dangling bulbs illuminate hawker stalls that serve up distinctive street food like curried noodles (*mie Aceh*) and steamed clams (*kerang rebus*).

This *ruko* or shophouse stands out with its easy blend of Art Deco and 1950s-style elements. Each floor stages and interplay between flavors. Recently spruced up, it looks set to remain standing for the foreseeable future. Despite the area's general shabbiness, Peunayong has maintained its commercial prowess now drawing Acehnese traders and tenants who trade in what were once largely Chinese properties

UNIVERSITAS IBA

YAYASAN IBA

Front elevation of the Universitas IBA, Palembang.

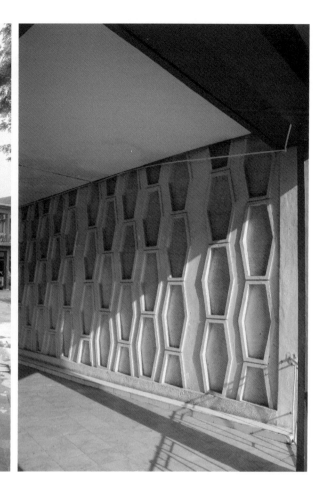

LEFT TO RIGHT: Examples of motif used extensively in porticos and corridors in the main teaching block.

Universitas IBA
Jalan Bangau, Palembang

ISriwijaya College became Palembang's first academy of higher learning in 1953. Ibu Ida and Bapak Bajumi, a prominent couple from Palembang, embarked on an ambitious plan to help educate the city's underprivileged children. The inauguration of Sriwijaya University in 1960 was closely followed by the IBA School (a portmanteau taken from the couple's first names).

The school's main wings were designed in a functional modern style using grid-like panels, yet there was thought given to decoration. A honeycomb motif was used freely by Oen Poo Haw, the American trained local architect. He applied this liberally from building façades, to decorating classroom interiors, along shaded and breezy corridors and within stairwells. The school was once one of Palembang's modernist landmarks and in 1986 became Universitas IBA.

Detail of wing adjoining the main university building.

Detail of entrance with tilting canopy.

LEFT: Detail of upper floor corridor. RIGHT: Classroom detail with further use of the honeycomb motif.

Courthouse Annex
Jalan M. Rifai, Palembang

The Straits of Malacca narrow considerably at Palembang and are littered with countless uninhabited mangrove-fringed islands. This terrain provided hideouts for various maritime criminals, from groups smuggling commodities and luxury goods, to armed gangs boarding vessels to rob crews. This lawlessness gave Palembang a reputation as a pirate's den. Upriver, indigenous groups like the Ogan sustained a culture of violent crime, robbery and hold ups.

Palembang's Dutch native court — still remembered by the older generation as the *Landraad* — became a District Court after Independence. During the 1960s, the old courthouse was unable to handle the city's rising tide of criminal and civil cases. In 1971, a new courthouse complex was built – a dual structure consisting of a bland multi-storey courthouse and an unusual annex. Some twenty years later, the annex reprised many of the precepts popularized in the 1950s such as a corrugated roof line, a simple, unadorned window sequence and striking overhangs which recall Frank Lloyd Wright's desert style.

Railway bungalows with a seamless fusion of *Indische* and modernist elements. OPPOSITE: Another bungalow unit from the same row.

Railway Housing
Jalan M. Isa, Palembang

At Independence, Sumatra's three railway networks were in a perilous state and urgently required resuscitation. The repair of tracks and purchase of some new locomotives from America helped the South Sumatra Railway to resume hauling coal and other freight. After the fall of President Sukarno, the railway lost many personnel. Most railway men were members of trade unions linked to the Communist Party. Arrests by the military created severe disruptions and many of the detained were never heard of again.

During this unsteady period of renewal and crisis, the South Sumatra Railway secured funds to build high-style housing for its senior managers. A row of identical bungalows was put up during the 1960s. The *Indische* style was enhanced using 1950s elements like the off-center canopies, the V forming pillars and *faux* chimneys. Only three bungalows remain, but they still serve as housing for railway managers.

White Bungalow
Jalan Veteran, Padang

The secessionist army movement of the late 1950s was little deterrence to Padang's Minangkabau community. With their flair for trade, commodities continued to be shipped to markets through the Straits of Malacca and beyond. Wartime business created new wealth, stirring up demand for showy housing. In the post-Independence years, *Indische* revival style architecture often satisfied.

This villa, set amongst spacious grounds is typical of post-Independence areas of Padang. It was built for a wealthy trader in the early 1960s. Unusually, this bungalow avoids reviving the late colonial era repertoire. Compared with the more expressive 1950s building style, its unadorned exterior stands out as a sober counterpoint to prevailing architectural trends.

Komando Housing
Jalan Achmad Yani, Padang

The army was the leading state institution in Indonesia in the years following Independence. Its multi-functionality was called upon to also run newly nationalized industries. Jakarta sought further political control through the military apparatus after quelling army mutinies in Sumatra and Sulawesi in 1958. A new tranche of officers trained in Java were dispatched to keep the provinces loyal to Jakarta. In Padang, like other cities in Sumatra, the army's housing footprint expanded.

These barracks were built for mid-ranking officers. Forming part of a residential complex, they contain an assortment of familiar barrack-style buildings and an array of functional bungalows – all in shades of green. On occasion, some bungalows came with more contemporary treatments. The dominant feature of this bunga-low is the battered chimney-like pilaster.

The eclectic trader's villa with its heavy accretions from later years.
OPPOSITE: The more recognizable 1950s styled pavilion with modest accretions.

Holiday Villa
Jalan Panorama, Bukittinggi

Bukittinggi is a small hill town nestled in the folds of Sumatra's 1,000-mile-long Bukit Barisan mountain range. Regarded as the cultural capital of the Minangkabau people, the epicenter of West Sumatra has churned out a diaspora of eminent thinkers and leaders. Propelled by the migratory custom of *merantau*, they have left their mark all over Indonesia.

Bukittingi under the Dutch was the prosperous administrative capital, Forte de Kock. High above sea level, it was a desirable getaway for Padang's elite.

The Japanese Army followed briefly, shifting their Sumatran headquarters to the hill town. After the fall of Yogjakarta to Dutch forces in 1948, Bukittingi served as the Indonesian Republic's emergency capital.

The 1950s — an era punctuated by war and peace — saw many bungalows and villas built according to the prevailing *Indische* revival trend. One of the few alternative builds, this holiday villa was built for a wealthy businessman opposite the cavernous Japanese war bunker attraction. As per

the tradition of moneyed households, it was built in two parts, the principal building for the family and a pavilion for guests. Both buildings went against the grain of prevailing fashions, but the pavilion stole the show with its relative restraint and simplicity, an oblique angled cut-away window sequence and a waving canopy with textured walls. Over the years, the main villa saw several accretions but the pavilion was largely spared.

Front elevation of the trader's mansion with its conspicuous shrine.

LEFT TO RIGHT: Detail of verandah and smooth rock cladding. Detail of air brick screen. Detail of the shrine.

Traders House
Jalan Raya Muntok

The global demand for tin in electronic equipment and gadgets will keep Bangka at the center of Indonesia's tin industry. Almost one hundred and fifty years ago a tin mining boom was started by a Dutch monopoly in Bangka's eastern port of Muntok and many Hakka Chinese from Batavia were shipped in. Soon indentured Chinese coolies, mostly from poor Hakka speaking communities in Southern China arrive in sizeable numbers to pick up the slack.

The Batavian Hakka were an older generation of settlers compared to recent mainland and Hong Kong arrivals. Working and living in close quarters while digging pits through the soft grey sandy soils, their co-mingling resulted in a new dialect. Bangka's Hakka dialect is almost unintelligible if spoken in South Sumatra, Riau, China or even next door in Belitung Island. After serving out their term of employment, indentured coolies were freed from labour contracts and could join a local association or *Kongsi*.

Freedom created a generation of eager tin traders, smugglers and entrepreneurs. This mansion, located on the edge of new Muntok is a colorful hybrid.

Built with a traditional double loggia, it exudes some 1950s-style trends popular in nearby Java and Sumatra. Fine rock accenting wraps the entire gable. The cladding extends down kinked verandah columns, patterned ventilation screens creating a cool space on the ground floor. The squat scarlet shrine guarding the house reflects a once ubiquitous practice from a distant homeland; reverence to the land deity. Much like this architecture, these practices reside with an older generation steadily disappearing.

The townhouse protected by its
defensive wall and iron gate.
OPPOSITE LEFT: Detail of restored
entrance and façade.
OPPOSITE RIGHT: View of the
guest room.

The Tan Villa
Jalan Ikan Gurame, Teluk Betung, Bandar Lampung

Set behind tall grey concrete walls is the mansion of once renowned businessman Tan Seng Beng. Born in South Sumatra in 1925, he first started in the family business trading cassava then other agricultural commodities. During the Japanese and Dutch occupations of the 1940s, he became pivotal to the independence struggle in South Sumatra. With his shrewd business skills, a command of several languages and his networks in Singapore, he ran a slick, but covert barter system, trading spices for guns and medicine.

The head of a large family, Pak Tan built a spacious and opulent mansion in the heart of Bandar Lampung's old town, Teluk Betung. Today it is easily overlooked, sandwiched between indistinct shophouse blocks. This was not the case in the early 1960s when its size and abundant glass windows were a statement.

Its sturdy iron gates were built for protection and to dissuade burglars who might be drawn to the property on one of the grandest streets in Teluk Betung. His house did become a target during the Chinese pogroms of late 1965 when mobs smashed much of this prized glass. His children can still remember the sound of bullets just outside their rooms. Pak Tan never imagined back in 1960 that its gates would withstand a truck attack, which is what happened during this period of chaos.

He was arrested and accused of being a communist sympathizer; a virtual death sentence. After a short detention and unexpected release, he installed iron bars to reinforce the gate. After years of calm in the 1980s, heeding the advice of a Feng Shui master, Pak Tan sealed the doorway to ward off evil spirits. Before his death he was persuaded by a rival Feng Shui master to reopen the mansion's original doorway. The last group of builders restored the distinctive flanging columns, but the tall gates remain.

Aannemer's Villa
Teluk Bitung, Bandar Lampung

In the 1920s, with just one university and two medical schools in the entire Dutch East Indies, tertiary education was an overseas enterprise for the extremely privileged. The more enlightened Dutch policy of *Concordantie* gave equal recognition to colonial education, opening the door — albeit very slightly — to a small number of local students aspiring to further study in the metropole. In the 1930s, Pak Siet Soen Fang was sent to Holland to study civil engineering. Upon his return to his home town of Teluk Betung he set up as a building contractor, putting his prestigious training to work, designing many distinguished properties including Bandar Lampung's principal Catholic Church, *Kristus Raja* (Christ the King).

This *Model Belanda* or Dutch inspired house was built by Pak Siet's as the family home in 1953. At first glance it resembles many Dutch-styled villas still standing in Java's former colonial quarters, (e.g. Menteng, Dago and Darmo). The villa makes an interesting, but subtle, departure with light touches of 1950s-style elements like the signature tilting wall and rock cladding. Still a family home, it is one of the few period buildings left in this part of Bandar Lampung.

Green Villa
Jalan Tenggiri, Teluk Bitung Bandar Lampung

IOver the last 20 years, the pace of economic life in Bandar Lampung's old town has dipped. New hillside malls have captured the latest phase in commerce and leisure, leaving Teluk Betung markedly quieter. Boarded-up cinemas and dining halls, rows of inactive shophouses and infrequently-used hotels signify its steady decline.

This two-storey townhouse is located on what was once a thriving road in the *Pecinan* quarter, and a quick journey to one of the oldest Confucian temples in South Sumatra, the Thay Hin Bio. Reflecting the wishes of the owner, a flowing panel of three *brise soliel* were fashioned to both protect and seclude its upper deck, maximizing privacy and preventing outsiders from seeing the goings-on inside. Empty for almost a decade, the villa was first passed onto the owner's children who subsequently sold it to an absentee owner.

KALIMANTAN

View of all six upper decks looking west.

Pertamina Villas

Jalan Cinta, Balikpapan

View of villas and grounds looking west

Alternate view of villas and grounds looking east.

Found floating in the Sumatran swamps, the wax-like minyak bumi (lit. earth oil) was traditionally used to treat muscle pains, fuel for lanterns and to caulk boats. In the 1880s a Dutch planter sensed a larger opportunity and began prospecting for oil. Discoveries by Shell followed in Balikpapan and across British Borneo. Royal Dutch and Shell merged to create Bataafsche Petroleum Maatschappij. By restricting American oil companies, it became the colony's primary oil producer and later one of Indonesia's largest companies.

In 1945, Allied bombing had virtually destroyed the Gunung Dubs refinery in Balikpapan. After the Japanese surrender, Dutch personnel were brought back to repair the plant and resume operations. As production was gradually restored, a new housing complex on the company's hillside camp was built.

View of ground floor living room.

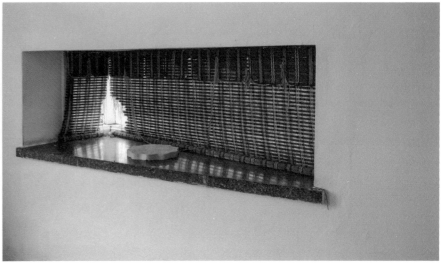

LEFT: Exterior detail of inverted geometric window. RIGHT: Interior detail of inverted geometric window.

This contained a fancy mix of Indische revival and 1950s-styled bungalows. At a nearby beachside location in Balikpapan, a variant of Ger Boom's influential Jakarta villas were reprised in the mid-1950s.

Built for Shell's senior managers, these freestanding villas were modelled closely on Ger Boom's Kebayoran Baru duplex prototype. Following a phase of oil industry consolidation in 1966, under Pertamina new refineries and townships were built.

The flair of these early designs was not repeated. These classics are now budget sector, no match for Balikpapan's downtown hotels and resorts

Former Shell bungalow from the late 1940s, Pertamina Gunung Dubs complex Balikpapan.

Former Shell bungalow in the 1950s style, Pertamina Gunung Dubs complex, Balikpapan.

Dayak Styled Villa
Jalan Achmad Yani, Banjarmasin

Banjarmasin, the coastal Malay port city, was founded near the confluence of the Barito and Martapura Rivers some 500 years ago. During the wet season, vast swathes of swampland form extensive lakes that lazily drain into the Java Sea. The city naturally evolved along a network of canals and waterways where goods and people moved by boat. Its many floating markets were once a common sight.

At the turn of the 20th century, artisans mining for gold and precious stones gave way to industrial-scale exploitation of natural resources. Rubber and coal were easily transported downriver on bamboo barges. Urbanization accelerated after Independence and Banjarmasin's once common waterways were filled to make way for roads.

Located in the old commercial district, this peculiar villa was fashioned in the spirit of lively experimentation. It deftly fuses late colonial-era designs with 1950s-style modernism. Its distinguishing feature is its three-feathered Dayak motif on the gable. Once used as a home for a local government official, it now stands derelict.

Air Force Housing
Syamsudin Noor Airport, Banjarmasin

As the Cold War reached a rolling boil in Asia, the USSR became the Indonesian Air Force or AURI's (*Angkatan Udara Republik Indonesia*) principal supplier of weaponry, including the much prized MIG fighter jet. Technical know-how was also provided by Russian personnel. By the early 1960s Indonesia had acquired air strike capability raising alarm in the west.

Bilateral ties with the USSR were abruptly severed after the 1965 coup and American re-alignment. In the early 1970s, Western aerospace companies began their move into the aircraft market. A once envied Soviet-supplied fleet was reduced to rusting aircraft parked at the ends of runways. A few were mounted on pylons to decorate airport entrances.

A more enduring legacy are the compounds of identical sky-blue bungalows, a common sight flanking Indonesia's older airports. At Banjarmasin's Syamsudin Noor International Airport, neat terraced rows of one-storey bungalows sport the characteristic sky blue AURI hue. These bungalows used simple mid-century modern inspired touches; walls tilt to create a pentagram trope and units were finished with exaggerated and sheared overhanging roofs, with contrasting white airway screens.

Emerald Villa

Jalan Ahmad Yani, Martapura

Over millennia, rocks bearing diamonds have washed into Kalimantan's large river basins like those emptying around Banjarmasin. The Dutch VOC propelled the diamond trade, helping to lay the foundations for Amsterdam as the world's premiere diamond-cutting and trading center. Kalimantan's diamond fields were never a match for the treasures excavated from the deep mines of Africa and India, yet for several centuries open sand pits have been shored up and gravels sifted in search of precious gems.

Mines around Martapura, an hour east of Banjarmasin, flourished after the Dutch relinquished their hold on the precious stone trade in the 1950s. Despite the smuggling of prized gems abroad, Martapura remains Indonesia's largest source of diamonds, amethysts and other semi-precious stones.

Located near Martapura's diamond market, this 1950s-period style villa, with its emerald hue, is one of those rare finds in a city characterized with much nondescript architecture from the New Order era. The villa's design shows the skills of an imaginative builder. Several elements create its brilliance – the heavily textured façade and gable, its sheared roof, the geometric set of canopies and an oddly reclining column shoring up the verandah.

Ex KODIM House

Jalan Panglima Batur, Muara Teweh

The riverside town of Muara Teweh sprang up around a Dutch fortress on the upper reaches of the snaking Barito River. It soon became home to coastal arrivals like the Banjar, Malay, Bakumpai as well as animist and Christian Dayak communities. By the late 1950s with law and order eroding fast, bandits took advantage of its relative isolation and scant security to rob barges, villages and camps.

To increase security, the army was organized into territorial commands, each *Komando Daerah Militer* (or Kodam) subdivided into KODIM (*Komando Distrik Militer*) stationed at village level. KODIM was badly needed in Muara Teweh and by the early 1960s they had built a modest complex of simple wooden houses near the old Dutch fort. Using local timber, these homes were somewhat distinguished by their urbane pentagonal façades. This left-over unit stands on legs similar to those seen on traditional floating houses on the muddy banks of Kalimantan's sinuous rivers. With improved security, the river outpost became a staging point to open up dense interiors. Once vast timber and rubber estates were displaced by coal - and more recently, mega scale palm oil plantations. Years after KODIM upgraded their facilities, the last of these wooden house was given over to rubbish collectors who recycle and sort town waste.

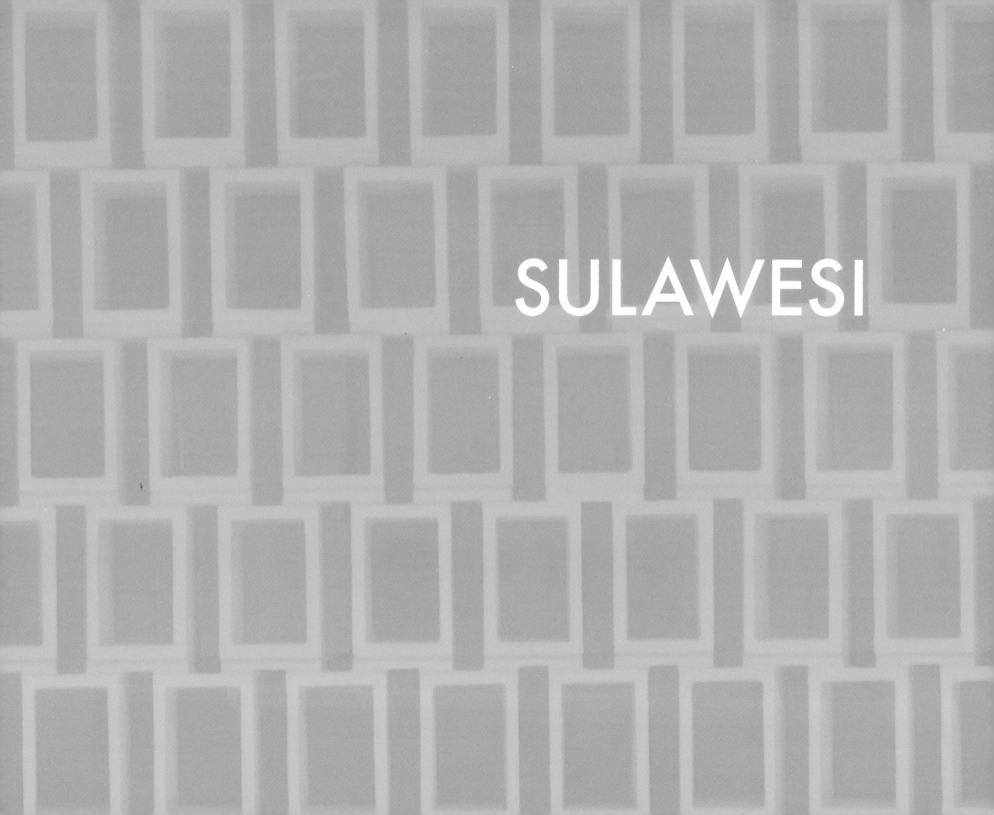

SULAWESI

Front elevation of the Haji villa with its checkered bay façade and futuristic car port.

The Haji Villa

Jalan Andi Mappanyuki, Makassar

After Independence, much of the interior of Sulawesi had fallen under the sway of lawlessness and banditry. An armed Islamist rebellion filled the void strangling the island's economic development and rendering the region one of Indonesia's poorest.

Haji Abdul Rashid, a Bugis trader bought copra in bulk from small holders in Southeast Sulawesi and sent his shipments across the Gulf of Bone to Makassar. This required exceptional navigational skills as his cargo passed through areas rife with dacoits and insurgents. Tasting commercial success, Pak Haji set about building his dream villa in Makassar in 1965. He hired a local building contractor who created a villa in a style that was in keeping with the city's wealthier families.

Rather than use the popular pentagram template, the contractor created a more distinctive design. He introduced an angular convex gable together with a unique space-age carport. Exterior texture was provided by a combination of traditional rockwork and *Indische* styled panels, above which is a small off-centre pentagram airway. The builder made several versions of this villa, both large and small, in central Makassar. Haji's, however, remains by far the best preserved and is let out by the family as a dental practice.

Partai Buruh Office
Jalan Urip Sumoharjo, Makassar

During the New Order years, only approved parties and state controlled unions were allowed to operate in Indonesia. In 1992, labor activist Muchtar Pakpahan began an underground union – the Confederation of Indonesian Prosperity Trade Unions. After gaining some popularity, he founded the Social Democrat Labor Party in 2001. Failing to secure even 1% of the vote, an undeterred Muchtar then formed Partai Buruh (the Worker's Party). To contest the 2009 elections, the new party opened offices in every province.

In South Sulawesi, the party office was located in eastern Makassar, an area developed in the early 1960s. Their regional office was a period villa designed when free trade unions and leftist parties were a recognized force. The single-storey property was a classic ensemble based on sparing architectural elements. Its signature feature is its oblique window canopy stretching to the ground. Apart from a coat of paint in the party's trademark blue and white, no modifications were made to their new office. Following another electoral disaster, the party was wound up in 2013 and the plot filled by a multi-storey block.

1950s Style Ruko
Jalan Urip Sumoharjo, Makassar

The largest metropolitan city in eastern Indonesia, Makassar, was for over a millennia the port that linked the expansive southern archipelago to Chinese shipping lanes. As the city expanded east in the late 1960s and 1970s, Jalan Urip Sumoharjo became a new commercial artery lined with modern looking shophouses that rivalled Makassar's old Chinatown quarter on the seafront.

Trading had modernized with the new Bugis and Makassarese mercantile community. The vibrant fusion of mid-century modern and Art Deco elements once helped business thrive at this ruko.

Stylistically, the oblique shaped window sequence and parapet corrugations clash with more muted Art Deco touches. Recently renovated, commercial hoardings now merge it with eastern Makassar's urban landscape

Oblique view of the school's main entrance.
OPPOSITE: A typical classroom interior.

School of Theology
Jalan Sam Ratulangi, Rantepao

Rantepao, high up in the folding hills of Sulawesi, is the cultural heartland of the Torajan people. At the beginning of the 20th century, the Dutch Protestant Church encouraged missionaries to tame and replace some traditional customs and animist belief systems. Over time conversions gathered pace, but defining aspects of Torajan customs or *adat* were retained. The missionary task was largely completed before Sulawesi's Islamic insurgency spread from the lowlands in the late 1950s.

Missionary work still required dedicated people to spread the faith. With security limited to Sulawesi's towns, Rantepao was chosen for the theological school where fresh pastors were trained to sustain the work of the Church. The school, located on tree-lined streets that once ringed Rantepao's Dutch quarter, was built following the everyday colonial-era style. Sparse 1950s architecturally themed elements make an appearance such as the tilted verandah and a prominent pentagram airway on the main façade. Still in use, it is now part of Universtas Kristen Indonesia.

Street view of the St. Ignatius Church.

Art Deco portal
window above
the 1950s-style
entrance.

LEFT: Crucifix themed window grilles. RIGHT: Stellar grilles above doorway.

Ignatius Catholic Church
Jalan Sudirman, Manado

Having secured its monopoly on trade in the early 17th century, the Dutch East Indies promoted Dutch Protestantism as the accompanying monopoly Western faith and kept Catholicism out of the colony. The ban on Catholicism was lifted during the first decade of the 19th century. The Jesuits, headquartered in Surabaya wasted little time and by the beginning of the 20th century had succeeded in making substantive conversions in eastern Indonesia's remote territories.

The political upheavals of the 1940s and 1950s ultimately led to the departure of Indonesia's small, but powerful European population. Yet, at the peak of President Sukarno's anti-Western policies, religion remained unaffected and Dutch pastors continued working in their churches.

In 1963, the streamlined Ignatius Catholic Church exemplified by its Art Deco-styled spire was built in

Manado. The flanging doorway and canopy below the Deco-styled circular window suggest an eclectic modernist hymn sheet. True to period eclecticism, elaborate grille ornamentation, redolent of the colonial-era decorate windows and panels above doors. The interior is functional in style; high set windows aid the cross flow of air and a row of suspended ceiling fans add vintage charm.

ACKNOWLEDGEMENTS

Retronesia was seven years in the making and could not have been possible without a constant flow of advice and suggestions from the following friends:

Frances Affandy, Sumur Sutrisno, Adji Damais, Adolf Heuken, Nadia Purwestri, Ria Febrian, Budi Lim, Scott Merrillees, John McGlynn, Robert McDonough, Jeremy Gross, Daniel Ziv, Mark Hanusz, and Karen Albans.

A larger group of people also deserve my gratitude for their hands-on assistance: those numerous owners, caretakers and real estate agents who kindly opened gates, doorways, moved parked cars, took down banners or hacked down trees and hedges to help me take my photographs.

WEST JAVA & JAKARTA

Bandung
Frances Affandy and Bandung Heritage, Ade Bagus, Sumur Sutrisno, Max Boenardi, Ibu Leni, Josep Saputra, David Braga, David Soegiri, Pak Daud, Adolf Heuken, Jenny Tanuwidjaja, Budi Tana, Henry Gunawan Tjhi, Hans Pol, Fauzan Noe'man, Myra Gunawan.

Bogor
Setiadi Sopandi, Christa Hardjasaputra, Guntur Santoso, Clarita Sarkar, FX Puniman.

Jakarta
Nadia Purwestri, Ria Febrian, Bambang Eryudhawan, Arya Arbeta, Budi Sukada, Han Awal, Harry Kwee, Adolf Heuken, Scott Merrillees, Amir Siddartha, Firmansyah, Priscilla Epifania, Rizka and Render Digital, Firman Lubis, Farida Lubis and family, Firman Santoso and family, Rudy Yuwono, Ibu Dewi Muharam and Pak Albert.

Cirebon
Leva Chendra and Irma.

CENTRAL JAVA

Semarang
Adji Damais, Prof. Totok Rusmanto, Ibu Widja Wijayanti, Anastasia Dwirahmi, Pak Hadi, Mas Ferry, Erastiany Asikin, Bob Hage, Lianita Zuhaeli, Yuki Namedya.

Kopeng
Warren de Jisrechg, Guntur Santoso, Mas Dedy Sonic, Yuki Namedya.

Yogyakarta
Yulianto Qin, Veronika Sawitri, Yuki Namedya, Annissa Gultom.

Magelang
Adolf Hueken, Kiki Post.

Solo
Sekar Pembayun, Dr Leni, Guru Adi, Adji Damais, Mas Bembi, Guru, Yulianto Qin, Henky Herendra, Daradjadi Gondodiprojo, Yuki Namedya.

EAST JAVA

Gresik
Graeme Steel, ITS Alumni, Rendy, Fauzi et al, Pak Gaguk, Yuki Namedya.

Surabaya

Graeme Steel, Prof Silas, Prof Josep,
ITS Alumni Rendy, Fauzi et al,
Liesbet Middelhoven-Rem, Oei Hiem Hwie,
Yuki Namedya.

Malang

Dr Melanie Budianta, FX Sisco, Mas Engga,
Ng Swan Ti, Nova Ruth, Doni Ukik,
Yuki Namedya, Les Smith.

Lawang

Yosep Adiyanto, Dr Melanie Budianta,
FX Sisco, Ng Swan Ti, Mas Engga,
Yuki Namedya.

—
SUMATRA

Aceh

Yenny Rahmayati, Mbak Hisan,
Jeremy Gross.

Medan

Suhardi Hartono, Irma Novrianty Nasution,
Yenny Rahmayati, Shindi Indira, Yuki Namedya.

Palembang

Yosep Adiyanto, Putry Athfi,
Bagus Wudiyanto, Aditya Dwi Laksana,
Adep, Yuki Namedya, Les Smith.

Bukittingi & Padang

Suharmedi and Prof Eko Alvares.

Bangka

Siong Kang and Budi Sukada.

Bandar Lampung

Leva Chendra, Liny Haryanto,
Mas TP, Tang Seng Beng Family and
Siet Soen Fang Family.

—
KALIMANTAN

Balikpapan

Bayu Prakosa, Sista Hapsari,
Colin Anderson, and Les Smith.

Banjarmasin

Les Smith, Martin Hughes, and
Robert McDonough.

Muara Teweh

Les Smith, Martin Hughes, and
Robert McDonough.

Martapura

Les Smith and Robert McDonough.

Pontianak

Heri Chendra and Ahmad Roffi.

—
SULAWESI

Makassar

Ria Wikantari, Adji Damais, Pak Nasir,
Haji Family, Jeremy Gross, Abdul Harris,
Basrie Kembang.

Rantepao

Abdul Harris and Adolf Heuken.

Manado

Adolf Heuken and Pak Albert.

—
THE EAST

Bali

Ketut Rana, Budi Sukada, Catrini,
Rumawan Putu.

Lombok

Tiwi and family, Ibu Widja Wijayanti.

Sorong

Wick Aliston

Ternate

Maulana Ibrahim

NOTES

WEST JAVA & JAKARTA

Kebayoran Baru Selection Jakarta
Freek Colombijn, Under Construction:
The Politics of Urban Space and Housing During
the Decolonization of Indonesia, 1930-1960.
KITLV Press 2010; Ministry of Public Works and
Power, Pembangunan Kota Baru Kebajoran,
June 1953. Suharmedi and Prof Eko Alvares.

BPI, Universitas ITB Bandung
Gm. Meyling Archive, NAI Rotterdam. Ilmu Alam
Indonesian Journal for Natural Sciences, Volume
112, Part II July–December 1956.

Poltekes Bandung
E. Ross Jenny, Public Health in Indonesia Public
Health Reports, Vol. 68, No. 4, April 1953; Vivek
Neelakantan, Health and Medicine in Soekarno
Era Indonesia: Social Medicine, Public Health
and Medical Education, 1949 to 1967 History &
Philosophy of Science, PhD Thesis University of
Sydney 2014.

Unpar Merdeka Campus Bandung
http://www.unpar.ac.id/tentang-unpar/sejarah/

CENTRAL JAVA

Kopeng Resort Kopeng
Mark & Bertie Uittenbogaard, Kopeng Notes.

Apotek Sputnik Semarang
Irawan Hudan, Nuky Krishna Rajasa & Teddy
Kurniawan, *Oei Tjong An, Sosok dan Karya*,
UNDIP Thesis 1995.

Museum Perjuangan Yogyakarta
Buku Panduan Museum Perjuangan,
Museum Perjuangan 2002.

Gereja St. Ignatius Magelang
*Gereja St. Ignatius Magelang Menampilkan
Wajahnya*, Kenangan 110 Tahun Gereja
St Ignatius Magelang, 2010.

EAST JAVA

Wisma Achmad Yani Gresik
Marshall Goldman, *A Balance Sheet of Soviet
Foreign Aid*, Journal of Foreign Affairs,
January 1965; http://www.foreignaffairs.com/
articles/23674/marshall-igoldman/a-balance-
sheet-ofsoviet-foreign-aid

The Furniture Store Gresik
Françoise Gipoloux Edward, *The Asian
Mediterranean Port cities and Trading networks
in China Japan and South East Asia 13th- 21st
century*, Elgar Publishing, 2011.

Hotel Olympic Surabaya
Howard W. Dick, *Surabaya: City of Work: A
Socioeconomic History*, 1900-2000. Singapore
University Press, 2003.

The Maritime Villa Malang
Chee Kiong Tong, *Identity and Ethnic Relations in
Southeast Asia: Racializing Chineseness*, Springer
2010; Malang Mignon: *Cultural Expressions of
the Chinese*, 1940- 1960, in Jennifer Lindsay and
Maya Liem (eds), *Heirs to World Culture, Being
Indonesian in 1950-1965*, Brill, 2012.

The Sarangan Villa Malang
*Malang Mignon: Cultural Expressions of the
Chinese, 1940- 1960*, in Jennifer Lindsay
and Maya Liem (eds), *Heirs to World Culture,
Being Indonesian in 1950-1965*, Brill, 2012.

The Veteran's House Malang
Yuli Krisna, *Why Indonesia's Veterans Must Not
Be Forgotten*, Jakarta Post Aug 17, 2013.

SUMATRA

Banker's Villa Kopeng
Thomas Lindblad and Peter Post, *Indonesian economic decolonization in regional and international perspective*, KITLV 2009.

DEKOPIN Medan
Robby Tulus, *Rediscovering the prominence of cooperatives*, The Jakarta Post Op Ed., July 19 2010.

Universitas IBA Palembang
William H. Frederick and Robert L. Worden, *Indonesia A country study*, Federal Research Division Library of Congress 2001; http://iba. ac.id/

Bungalow Padang
Suharmedi Ragam, *Bentuk Rumah Bergaya 'Jengki' di Kota Padang*, Master Thesis, Universitas Bung Hatta 2010.

KALIMANTAN

Pertamina Balikpapan
Daniel Yergin The Prize: The Epic Quest for Oil, Money & Power, Simon & Schuster, 2012.

Airforce Housing Banjarmasin
Harry G Shaffer, *A collection of western and Soviet views The Soviet Economy*: 1940–1965, Meredith Corporation 1969; Foreign Affairs, Guy J Pauker 1962, *The Soviet Challenge in Indonesia*, http://www.foreignaffairs.com/articles/23427/guy-j-pauker/ the-soviet-challenge-inindonesia.

Banjarmasin Vila Banjarmasin
Harold Brookfield et al, *In Place of the Forest: Environmental and socioeconomic transformation in Borneo and the Eastern Malay Peninsula*, United Nations University Press, 1995.

Martapura Vila Martapura
L.K Spencer et al, *The Diamond Deposits of Kalimantan*, Borneo, Gems & Gemology Summer, 1988.

Ex Kodim Muara Teweh
Taufiq Tanasaldy, *Regime Change and Ethnic Politics in Indonesia: Dayak politics of West Kalimantan*, KITLV 2012; Angel Rabasa and Peter Chalk, *Indonesia's Transformation and the Stability of Southeast Asia*, Rand Corporation, 2001.

SULAWESI

The Haji Villa Makassar
Audrey Kahin & George Kahin, *Subversion as Foreign Policy: The Secret Eisenhower and Dulles Debacle in Indonesia*, The New Press, 1995.

1950s Style Ruko Makassar
Julian Davison, *Singapore Shophouse*, Talisman Publishing, 2010.

Sekolah Teologi Tinggi Rantepao
Roxana Waterson, *Paths and Rivers Sa'dan Toraja Society in Transformation*, KITLV 2009.

Gereja Katolik Ignatius Manado
Karel Steenbrink, *Catholics in Indonesia 1808-1942 A Documented History*, KITLV.

ABOUT THE AUTHOR

TARIQ KHALIL

lives and works in Indonesia. His photographs—always about buildings and their histories—have been exhibited as solo and group shows in London, across the rest of the UK, Dubai, Jakarta, and Athens. For some seven years Tariq has taken whatever opportunity has come his way to make Retronesia. It is his most ambitious project to date and has featured in *Kompas*, Indonesia's national daily newspaper. Tariq is a regular columnist for *Indonesia Design* magazine on all things *retro*.

CPSIA information can be obtained at www.ICGtesting.com
Printed in the USA
BVIW12n2127030518
515187BV00019B/287